PERSONALITY *Plus* FOR PARENTS

Other books by Florence Littauer

Personality Plus

Personality Puzzle with Marita Littauer

Put Power in Your Personality!

Getting Along with Almost Anybody with Marita Littauer

Talking So People Will Listen with Marita Littauer

Shades of Beauty with Marita Littauer

Why Do I Feel the Way I Do? with Fred Littauer

Daily Marriage Builders with Fred Littauer

After Every Wedding Comes a Marriage with Fred Littauer

Freeing Your Mind from Memories That Bind with Fred Littauer

Taking Charge of Your Life

How to Beat the Blahs

Blow Away the Black Clouds

It Takes So Little to Be above Average

How to Get Along with Difficult People

Out of the Cabbage Patch

I've Found My Keys, Now Where's My Car?

Silver Boxes

Dare to Dream

Raising Christians, Not Just Children

Your Personality Tree (also available as video album)

Hope for Hurting Women

Looking for God in All the Right Places

The Gift of Encouraging Words

Get a Life without the Strife with Fred Littauer

PERSONALITY *Plus* FOR PARENTS

Understanding What Makes Your Child Tick

FLORENCE LITTAUER

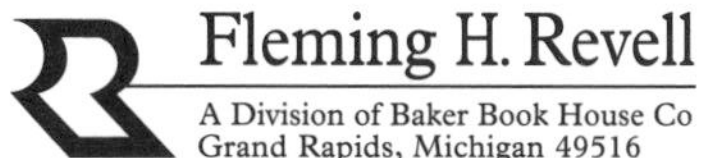
Fleming H. Revell
A Division of Baker Book House Co
Grand Rapids, Michigan 49516

Published by Fleming H. Revell
a division of Baker Book House Company
P.O. Box 6287, Grand Rapids, MI 49516-6287

Printed in the United States of America

Library of Congress Cataloging-in-Publication Data

Littauer, Florence, 1928–
Personality plus for parents : understanding what makes your child tick / Florence Littauer.
p. cm.
Includes bibliographical references
ISBN 0-8007-5737-8 (pbk.)
1. Personality in children. 2. Temperament in children. 3. Child rearing—Religious aspects—Christianity. I. Title.

BF723.P4 L58 2000
155.4'182—dc21 00-037279

For current information about all releases from Baker Book House, visit our web site:
http://www.bakerbooks.com

CONTENTS

INTRODUCTION

"I Don't Know What's Wrong with My Child!"

Fred and I were enjoying a quiet Sunday brunch at the restaurant in our hotel when the hostess seated a family—parents, grandparents, and ten-month-old child—at a nearby table. As they settled into their seats, we couldn't help but watch the commotion.

The child clearly didn't want to sit in the high chair that was pulled up to the table. Her screams of protest made that evident! But all her squirming and squealing didn't stop her determined mother from firmly placing her in the chair anyway.

Meanwhile the father quietly slid into his seat and began to browse the menu, while the grandparents exchanged a wary glance before taking their seats. Soon the whole family was seated and the adults were ready to enjoy a nice meal. The child, however, had a different idea.

Every few minutes she would point upward and let out a bone-chilling shriek that caught the attention of every person in the restaurant. The flustered mother quickly scrambled to placate the little one with a few crackers. Immediately the child crushed each cracker into pieces, gathered them into a pile, then picked them up and tossed them into the air. She screamed in delight as the flakes fell on her and the table.

At this point the mother slumped in her chair and sighed. "I don't know what to do with her anymore," she admitted to her parents.

The grandmother shook her head. "I don't know either, dear. You were never like that," she said.

"Your mother's right. You were always quiet and well behaved," the grandfather added. "We could take you anywhere and you never made a scene."

With a glance at her husband, who was hunched over in his chair still studying the menu, the mother raised her hands in an apologetic gesture and said, "I just don't know what's wrong with her!"

Does this story sound familiar to you? Have you ever wondered why your child doesn't act as you expect him to act? why one child is loud, boisterous, and full of fun while another is quiet, obedient, analytical, and perfectionistic from the beginning? why one is strong, active, and controlling of the entire family and another is compliant, friendly, peaceful, and no trouble at all?

This book will help you answer those questions and bring harmony to your home.

Like the cast for a Broadway show, the members of your family play various roles and must work together to produce a successful blend. Unlike the Broadway cast, however, your family members don't audition for their roles. Couples meet and marry without evaluation by an experienced casting director, and we don't choose some children and send others packing based on how well they fit a role. Instead, we must learn to understand the cast we have and work with it.

In this book I will show you and your cast how to use the concept of the four basic personalities to understand yourself and to learn how to get along with each person in your family. You'll begin to see why your child acts the way he does and how you as a parent should respond. Rather than worrying about why Suzy Sanguine talks all the time and forgets her chores, why Charlie Choleric bosses his friends around and seems to control even you, why Martin Melancholy is so neat and organized but easily hurt, or why Phyllis Phlegmatic is so relaxed and doesn't seem to care about any of your exciting plans, you can train your child according to the pattern God has established in his personality. The resulting production is sure to be a smashing success!

PART 1

Overview of the Personalities

one

WHAT ARE THE PERSONALITIES?

It doesn't take long for a parent to realize that not all children act alike, but we seldom know what to do about it. One child may be bubbly and outgoing while another is reserved and withdrawn. One may demand constant attention while another is content to be left on her own.

When her triplets were four years old, Cheryl gathered them around the table to decorate gingerbread men. After dividing the cookies evenly and placing bowls of frosting, gumdrops, candy sprinkles, and M&M's on the table, she watched as the three little ones began to create their masterpieces.

Bryce dove right in, slathering frosting with wild abandon and cramming as many pieces of candy as possible onto each cookie. He also couldn't help but sneak a cookie or two into his mouth. His uncontrolled behavior disturbed his sister Sarah Jean, who pleaded, "Mommy, make him stop! He's using all the candy! I get the pink and purple gumdrops 'cause I'm the girl!" At Sarah Jean's protest, Cheryl stepped in to divide all the candies equally before Bryce had indeed used all of the colorful pieces.

Meanwhile, despite the commotion created by his siblings, Blake was carefully studying his cookies and the various decorations available to him. He hadn't even started to decorate. When asked if he needed help, he explained, "I need help making the face right." Despite his mother's encouragement to just decorate the cookies any way he wanted, Blake refused to begin until she agreed to help him form eyes, nose, mouth, and hair for the first gingerbread man. Blake then completed the decoration, adding just a single, perfectly centered M&M button to the body. With that perfect cookie completed, Blake saw no reason to continue decorating others. So he asked his mother to wipe his hands so he could go do something else. As he scampered off to play with his Legos, Bryce volunteered, "I'll take his candy!" to which Sarah Jean squawked, "No! Mommy! Divide them!"[1]

Despite the common bond these three children share as triplets—same parents, same home environment, same food, same stories—their approaches to this project differed drastically. Impetuous Bryce was interested in having as much fun as possible with his colorfully decorated cookies. Orderly Sarah Jean demanded that everything be done fairly and on her terms. And cautious Blake was determined to produce the perfect specimen on his first try.

So what makes each child so different?

Born to Be Unique

Studies have confirmed that children are born with prepackaged personalities that largely determine how they will interact with the world around them. Environment does play a role in the expression of a person's inborn personality, but the existence of a personality that is present from birth is undeniable.

In 1979 the University of Minnesota began a study called "Twins Reared Apart." The study revealed convincing evidence that personality is inherited. By bringing together and testing twins who had been separated at birth, adopted into different families, and brought up with no contact, the university team concluded that we inherit more of our adult behavior than was previously imagined. Twins in the study were dumbfounded to meet exact replicas of themselves in looks, mannerisms, attitudes, sociability, and personality.

A similar study at Indiana University generated the same results. Individuals whose only link during childhood had been their genetic makeup grew up to be remarkably similar in every way.

I've personally met a number of twins at my seminars who have related stories confirming their inborn similarities. Janette and Annette, for example, were born seven minutes apart. Both married evangelists and twice gave birth to babies at the same time. Though they live eight hundred miles apart, they frequently do the same things on the same day, only later discovering their identical actions.

Lana and Lorna, separated at birth and later reunited, found when they visited each other that they had chosen the same wallpaper for their master bedrooms and had many of the same outfits in their closets. Another pair told me that after being apart for thirty years they came together to discover that both of them were writing and illustrating children's books.

As these stories indicate, humans inherit far more than just physical characteristics such as eye and hair color. Rather, we come preprogrammed with a direction of response to life that causes shyness, aggressive action, happiness, depression, talkativeness, desire to control, and many other traits.

The biological makeup of individuals is complex, but genes clearly influence our responses. Individuals react to similar experiences in surprisingly similar or different ways, depending on their inborn personality traits. Author Dean Hamer concludes, "You have about as much choice in some aspects of your personality as you do in the shape of your nose or the size of your feet."[2]

Since we can't choose our personalities—or those of our children—what's left for us to do is to identify and work with the personalities we've been given. Before we can follow Scripture's admonition to "train a child in the way he should go" (Prov. 22:6), we must gain an understanding and respect for each child's individuality. To do that we need to understand the four basic personality types that characterize all people—adults and children.

The Basics—Four Possibilities

More than two thousand years ago, around 400 B.C., Greek scholars sought to explain the differing natures they observed in human beings. Hippocrates, now called the father of modern medicine, theorized that what made people so different from each other were the chemicals in their bodies. He identified four bodily fluids—blood, yellow bile, phlegm, and black bile—that he believed gave rise to a person's behaviors.

Centuries later, around A.D. 149, a Roman physiologist by the name of Galen proposed a temperament theory that built on Hippocrates' observations. According to Galen, four basic human personalities—Sanguine, Choleric, Melancholy, and Phlegmatic—were possible, depending on the amount of each bodily fluid, or "humor," in a person's body.

In recent years psychologists have reexamined these ideas and discovered that, while the ancient Greeks and Romans didn't get everything right, there is more truth in their theories than was once supposed. Although the four humors identified by our ancient friends don't really cause behavioral differences in humans, four basic personalities can be used to categorize people. And we've chosen to use the same Greek terms to describe these four basic personalities.

The Popular Personality—Sanguine

Popular Sanguines are high-energy, fun-loving, outgoing people. They are the ones with the bumper stickers on their cars asking, "Are we having fun yet?"

Sanguines seek the attention, affection, approval, and acceptance of those around them. These boisterous individuals bring fun and drama into almost any situation, love the spotlight, and enjoy motivating others. They initiate conversations and can instantly become best friends with everyone in a group. Sanguines are usually optimistic and almost always charming. However, they can be disorganized, emotional, and hypersensitive about what others think of them.

Of a Sanguine person you might make comments such as, "She talks all the time" or "He never met a stranger." You may call this person the "talker."

The Powerful Personality—**Choleric**

Powerful Cholerics are those who are naturally goal-oriented, who live to achieve, and who organize quickly. Their motto would echo the Nike advertising slogan "Just do it."

Cholerics seek loyalty and appreciation from others. They strive for control and expect credit for their achievements. They love being challenged and easily accept difficult assignments. Their self-discipline and ability to focus make them strong leaders. But their drive and determination can cause them to become workaholics, make them opinionated and stubborn, and leave them insensitive to others' feelings.

Of the Choleric you may say, "He really gets in your face" or "If you want to get something done, ask her." You would call this person the "doer."

The Perfect Personality—Melancholy

The Perfect Melancholy is quieter, deeper, and more thoughtful than others. Melancholies strive for perfection in everything that is important to them. Their motto would be "If it's worth doing, it's worth doing right!" With perfection as their goal, these people are often disappointed and even depressed by less-than-perfect results.

Melancholies need sensitivity and support from others. And they require space and silence in which to think before they speak, write, or act. They are task-oriented folks who are careful and organized. These perfectionists thrive on order, and you can depend on them to complete a job on time. But their perfectionism may make them critical or pessimistic, and they drive themselves crazy with their efforts to measure up to their own high standards.

When speaking about the Melancholy you'll likely say, "She is so together" or "He is such a perfectionist." You might call this person a "thinker."

The Peaceful Personality—**Phlegmatic**

Peaceful Phlegmatics are balanced, contented people. They don't feel compelled to change the world or to upset the status quo. The original conservationists, they view all of life through the filter of conserving their energy. Their motto might be "Why stand when you can sit? Why sit when you can lie down?" To the more driven personalities, Phlegmatics appear to be slower than the rest. This isn't because they *aren't* as smart as others; it's because they *are* smarter. While we fret and worry, they watch and determine not to "sweat the small stuff."

Phlegmatics dislike risk, challenge, and surprise and will require time to adapt to changes. Although they avoid situations that are too stressful, they can work well under pressure. However, their lack of discipline and motivation often allows them to procrastinate in the absence of a strong leader.

Phlegmatics are reserved, but they enjoy being around people. Although they don't have the need to talk as much as the Sanguine, they have an innate wit and seem to say the right thing at just the right time. They are steady and stable; and because they are security-oriented, they like to create safety for their spouses and children. They seek peace and quiet and tend to act as negotiators instead of fighters. These loyal individuals find worth and respect in providing for their families and assisting people who need help.

When referring to the Phlegmatic, you would say things like, "She is so sweet" or "He is such a nice guy." You would view this person as a "watcher."

The following chart summarizes the basic characteristics of each personality type:

Popular Sanguine Basic Desire: have fun Emotional Needs: attention affection approval acceptance Controls By: charm	LEAD Extroverted • Optimistic • Outspoken	**Powerful Choleric** Basic Desire: have control Emotional Needs: loyalty sense of control appreciation credit for work Controls By: threat of anger
PLAY Witty • Easygoing • Not goal-oriented		WORK Decisive • Organized • Goal-oriented
Peaceful Phlegmatic Basic Desire: have peace Emotional Needs: peace and quiet feeling of worth lack of stress respect Controls By: procrastination	ANALYZE Introverted • Pessimistic • Soft-spoken	**Perfect Melancholy** Basic Desire: have perfection Emotional Needs: sensitivity support space silence Controls By: threat of moods

Partnering Personalities

Every person is born with a predisposition toward one (or more) of these four personality types. Most of us are a combination of two personalities. Sometimes they are balanced evenly, but usually one is predominant.

There are four natural combinations of personalities that occur when any two adjoining squares are combined from the personality chart on page 19. The top two cells—Sanguine and Choleric—combine naturally because both types are extroverted, optimistic, and outspoken. This combination results in a highly excitable individual who is energized by people. Sanguine/Choleric children are charming and talkative while getting their work done, either by themselves or, often, by getting others to do it for them.

The Melancholy and Phlegmatic cells at the bottom of the chart combine well because both personalities are introverted, pessimistic, and soft-spoken. A Melancholy/Phlegmatic will be less excitable and more drained by people. When my Melancholy son was about six, I greeted him early in the morning with, "How are you today?" He answered, "All right, so far. I haven't run into any people yet." It's dealing with people that wears out these individuals. At their best, Melancholy/Phlegmatics do things perfectly and on time while being pleasant and nonconfrontational. At times, however, their nit-picking nature will leave them depressed and too drained to accomplish anything.

Because the two sides of their personalities have so many traits in common, the Sanguine/Choleric and Melancholy/Phlegmatic combinations are usually quite balanced between the two types. In contrast, Choleric/Melancholy or Sanguine/Phlegmatic combinations join an optimist with a pessimist, an excitable with an unexcitable individual and a people person with a reserved one. Consequently they tend to be less balanced, leaving a personality that is predominantly one or the other. Individuals with these combinations may swing in and out of two personalities according to the circumstances.

The personalities on the right side of the chart—Choleric and Melancholy—combine to produce a highly task-focused individual. This combination will be the greatest achiever, doing things quickly while wanting everything to be perfect. But they may become bossy and manipulative while being discouraged that no one does anything right or on time.

The Sanguine and Phlegmatic personalities on the left side of the chart also combine easily, resulting in a very relationship-oriented person. This combination makes everyone's favorite friend—Sanguine fun with an agreeable and easygoing Phlegmatic nature. The Sanguine/Phlegmatic, adorable with a great sense of humor, is always relaxed and accepts you as you are. They may tend, though, to be undisciplined or sarcastic and unwilling to *do* anything. They easily forget their responsibilities but can always charm someone else into doing them.

Can Opposites Be One?

Each of us was born with a particular personality or natural combination, but some individuals seem to display traits of apparently opposite personalities. You may see yourself as a Peaceful Phlegmatic at home but a Powerful Choleric as soon as you step into the office. Or perhaps you find yourself compulsively organizing things, as you'd expect from a Perfect Melancholy, but your favorite pastime is performing on center stage as the life of the party. How can that be? Do opposite personalities really combine?

While it's true that many people *function* in opposing personalities, most often such individuals don't really *possess* such a personality. In some cases, we actually attribute certain characteristics to the wrong personality type. Without completely understanding both the behavior and the motivation for each personality, we find ourselves assuming that only Melancholies are organized (although Cholerics can be as well) and that only Cholerics can be strong leaders (although others can learn to be such).

Also, many of us can find areas of our lives in which we've learned to act in a certain way, regardless of our natural tendency in the situation. In short, to discover our true personality we must learn to distinguish between the *natural self* and the *trained self.* When we don't, we leave ourselves in a position of operating in a personality that is not really our own. In doing so, we put on a mask that hides our true personality, projects a false one, and ultimately wears us out.

Wearing Masks

Masking is a term we use to represent the behavior of a person who is not functioning in his or her birth personality. When we aren't being who we were created to be, our whole life is like being in a play. We are acting out a part that isn't real, and ultimately this exhausts us. What causes masking?

Avoiding Rejection

From the time we are born, our basic instincts include fear of rejection and need for acceptance. For this reason, children may shift their personality if they have experienced rejection, or even a lack of acceptance, by those they love. Abused children, for example, may try to change their personalities to be whatever they perceive will please their abusers. They think, "If I'm quiet . . . if I smile more . . . if I do my chores perfectly . . . then I won't be hurt anymore."

Meeting Expectations

When children are repeatedly expected to act in a certain way, they often live up to the expectations. So parents who knowingly or unknowingly predetermine what a child should be like can alter that child's personality. By trying to raise children who live up to the parents' hopes and expectations, parents can alter their children's opinions of who they really are. Some have even pushed so hard that their kids find themselves in careers that please their parents but that they don't enjoy and that don't fit their personalities.

Melancholy Joyce determined to be the perfect mother and to produce a perfect child molded in her image. Countless times she instructed, "Shh, use your quiet voice" or "I am not the entertainment committee." Not until her daughter was in high school did Joyce learn about the personalities and figure out that her daughter was a Sanguine who needed to relate to people by having fun with them. Once she knew this, she finally ceased her callous attempts to make her child into herself. Instead, she let her daughter blossom into her own person and discover the joys of being Sanguine. Had Joyce known about the personalities sooner, her daughter's childhood could have been much more fun for both mother and child.

Cookie-Cutter Parenting

Parents who don't understand the role of nature in their children may try to make every child act the same. "All children should be seen and not heard" may work well with your Melancholy and Phlegmatic children, but it will stifle the spontaneity of the Sanguine who says, "This is no fun!" and the leadership potential of the Choleric who protests, "Don't I have a vote here?"

Pat treated her two sons exactly the same despite their different personalities. She looked at her sons as a "package deal"—they looked alike, were both athletic, and had the same parents. Pat did as her mother had instructed her; she treated them both alike. Whatever Rick did, Rob followed: sports, lessons, and clubs. Pat prided herself on what a great mother she was to keep them equal. But when Rick went off to college, Rob announced,

"I'm taking a year off." When asked what he meant, he explained, "I'm taking a year off from being my brother. I've done what you wanted me to do; but now that he's gone, I need a year to rest up and find myself." Only when Pat learned about the personalities did she fully realize what Rob meant. He was a Melancholy/Phlegmatic who had been forced to play a Sanguine/Choleric like his brother. Pat is grateful that Rob had the sense to quit the game, take off the mask, and not remain part of the "package deal" forever.

Whatever the reason for the mask you or your child may wear, it's important to recognize your true personality and to learn to remove the mask that covers it. So how do you determine your true personality? Turn to the next chapter to find out.

two

PROFILING PARENT AND CHILD PERSONALITIES

What's My Personality Type?

By now you've probably begun to recognize yourself and others in the descriptions you've read. It doesn't take long before we begin to get an idea of which personality we're most like. Before we begin to analyze our children's personalities, it's important to take a look at ourselves. You'll probably notice that you and your spouse have opposite personalities. That's the way God planned for you to fill in each other's weaknesses and benefit from each other's strengths. Besides, your children don't really need two parents who are exactly alike! It's better for them to have a variety of role models to follow.

To determine exactly what blend of personality you are, use the profile questionnaire below. In each row of four words, place an X in front of the word (or words) that most often applies to you. Continue through all forty lines. If you're not sure which word most applies to you, ask your spouse or a friend to help you. Use the word definitions in appendix B for the most accurate results.

Personality Profile Questionnaire

Strengths

1	__ Adventurous	__ Adaptable	__ Animated	__ Analytical
2	__ Persistent	__ Playful	__ Persuasive	__ Peaceful
3	__ Submissive	__ Self-sacrificing	__ Sociable	__ Strong-willed
4	__ Considerate	__ Controlled	__ Competitive	__ Convincing
5	__ Refreshing	__ Respectful	__ Reserved	__ Resourceful
6	__ Satisfied	__ Sensitive	__ Self-reliant	__ Spirited
7	__ Planner	__ Patient	__ Positive	__ Promoter
8	__ Sure	__ Spontaneous	__ Scheduled	__ Shy
9	__ Orderly	__ Obliging	__ Outspoken	__ Optimistic
10	__ Friendly	__ Faithful	__ Funny	__ Forceful
11	__ Daring	__ Delightful	__ Diplomatic	__ Detailed
12	__ Cheerful	__ Consistent	__ Cultured	__ Confident
13	__ Idealistic	__ Independent	__ Inoffensive	__ Inspiring
14	__ Demonstrative	__ Decisive	__ Dry humor	__ Deep
15	__ Mediator	__ Musical	__ Mover	__ Mixes easily
16	__ Thoughtful	__ Tenacious	__ Talker	__ Tolerant
17	__ Listener	__ Loyal	__ Leader	__ Lively
18	__ Contented	__ Chief	__ Chart maker	__ Cute
19	__ Perfectionist	__ Pleasant	__ Productive	__ Popular
20	__ Bouncy	__ Bold	__ Behaved	__ Balanced

Weaknesses

21	__ Blank	__ Bashful	__ Brassy	__ Bossy
22	__ Undisciplined	__ Unsympathetic	__ Unenthusiastic	__ Unforgiving
23	__ Reticent	__ Resentful	__ Resistant	__ Repetitious
24	__ Fussy	__ Fearful	__ Forgetful	__ Frank
25	__ Impatient	__ Insecure	__ Indecisive	__ Interrupts
26	__ Unpopular	__ Uninvolved	__ Unpredictable	__ Unaffectionate
27	__ Headstrong	__ Haphazard	__ Hard to please	__ Hesitant
28	__ Plain	__ Pessimistic	__ Proud	__ Permissive

29	Angered easily	Aimless	Argumentative	Alienated
30	Naïve	Negative attitude	Nervy	Nonchalant
31	Worrier	Withdrawn	Workaholic	Wants credit
32	Too sensitive	Tactless	Timid	Talkative
33	Doubtful	Disorganized	Domineering	Depressed
34	Inconsistent	Introvert	Intolerant	Indifferent
35	Messy	Moody	Mumbles	Manipulative
36	Slow	Stubborn	Show-off	Skeptical
37	Loner	Lord over others	Lazy	Loud
38	Sluggish	Suspicious	Short-tempered	Scatterbrained
39	Revengeful	Restless	Reluctant	Rash
40	Compromising	Critical	Crafty	Changeable

Once you've completed the profile, transfer your answers to the scoring sheet that follows. Add up your total number of responses in each column and combine your totals from the strengths and weaknesses sections.

Personality Scoring Sheet

Strengths

	Popular Sanguine	Powerful Choleric	Perfect Melancholy	Peaceful Phlegmatic
1	Animated	Adventurous	Analytical	Adaptable
2	Playful	Persuasive	Persistent	Peaceful
3	Sociable	Strong-willed	Self-sacrificing	Submissive
4	Convincing	Competitive	Considerate	Controlled
5	Refreshing	Resourceful	Respectful	Reserved
6	Spirited	Self-reliant	Sensitive	Satisfied
7	Positive	Promoter	Planner	Patient
8	Spontaneous	Sure	Scheduled	Shy
9	Optimistic	Outspoken	Orderly	Obliging
10	Funny	Forceful	Faithful	Friendly
11	Delightful	Daring	Detailed	Diplomatic
12	Cheerful	Confident	Cultured	Consistent
13	Inspiring	Independent	Idealistic	Inoffensive

14	__ Demonstrative	__ Decisive	__ Deep	__ Dry humor
15	__ Mixes easily	__ Mover	__ Musical	__ Mediator
16	__ Talker	__ Tenacious	__ Thoughtful	__ Tolerant
17	__ Lively	__ Leader	__ Loyal	__ Listener
18	__ Cute	__ Chief	__ Chart maker	__ Contented
19	__ Popular	__ Productive	__ Perfectionist	__ Pleasant
20	__ Bouncy	__ Bold	__ Behaved	__ Balanced

Total—Strengths

________	________	________	________

Weaknesses

	Popular Sanguine	Powerful Choleric	Perfect Melancholy	Peaceful Phlegmatic
21	__ Brassy	__ Bossy	__ Bashful	__ Blank
22	__ Undisciplined	__ Unsympathetic	__ Unforgiving	__ Unenthusiastic
23	__ Repetitious	__ Resistant	__ Resentful	__ Reticent
24	__ Forgetful	__ Frank	__ Fussy	__ Fearful
25	__ Interrupts	__ Impatient	__ Insecure	__ Indecisive
26	__ Unpredictable	__ Unaffectionate	__ Unpopular	__ Uninvolved
27	__ Haphazard	__ Headstrong	__ Hard to please	__ Hesitant
28	__ Permissive	__ Proud	__ Pessimistic	__ Plain
29	__ Angered easily	__ Argumentative	__ Alienated	__ Aimless
30	__ Naïve	__ Nervy	__ Negative attitude	__ Nonchalant
31	__ Wants credit	__ Workaholic	__ Withdrawn	__ Worrier
32	__ Talkative	__ Tactless	__ Too sensitive	__ Timid
33	__ Disorganized	__ Domineering	__ Depressed	__ Doubtful
34	__ Inconsistent	__ Intolerant	__ Introvert	__ Indifferent
35	__ Messy	__ Manipulative	__ Moody	__ Mumbles
36	__ Show-off	__ Stubborn	__ Skeptical	__ Slow
37	__ Loud	__ Lord over others	__ Loner	__ Lazy
38	__ Scatterbrained	__ Short-tempered	__ Suspicious	__ Sluggish
39	__ Restless	__ Rash	__ Revengeful	__ Reluctant
40	__ Changeable	__ Crafty	__ Critical	__ Compromising

Total—Weaknesses

________	________	________	________

Combined Totals

_________ _________ _________ _________

Now you're able to see your dominant personality type. You'll also see what combination of personalities you are. If, for example, your score is 35 in Powerful Choleric strengths and weaknesses, there's really little doubt. You're nearly all Powerful Choleric. But if your score is, for example, 16 in Powerful Choleric, 14 in Melancholy, and 5 in each of the others, you're a Powerful Choleric with a strong Perfect Melancholy personality also.

You'll find an extra copy of this test and scoring sheet in appendix B. Make copies of it and take some family time for each member of your household to fill it out. For young children, the test will serve only as a starting point. You'll need profiles in a later section of this chapter to clearly identify your child's personality. But first, take a look at your scoring sheet and the terms that describe you and consider how those results affect your parenting style.

What Kind of Parent Are You?

Now that you've identified your own unique strengths and weaknesses, you'll be better able to understand yourself as a parent and why you get along with one child better than you do with another.

The Popular Parent (Sanguine)

The Popular parent loves to have fun and thrives on an audience. Children may become the audience for a Sanguine mother who turns on her stage personality when her child's friends arrive. She'll play games with the children, but since Sanguines get self-worth from the response of those around them, a disinterested group of children will cause the parent to turn off the charm. After all, why bother being cute and adorable if no one cares?

When I met Yole at a party, she reminded me of a time ten years earlier when she had come to me asking for help. She had heard me speak on the personalities and wondered why she couldn't get along with her son. Yole, a bright-eyed, adorable Sanguine, had a Melancholy son of six. As we talked about him, I quickly saw that he did not respond to Yole's humor. She got angry as she told me about the hilarious thing she'd done that he had refused even to notice. She wanted to be the clever comedian, but her audience appeared to be bored or humiliated.

There's no worse punishment for the Sanguine parent than to be ignored by the family. When I shared this thought with Yole, she realized that she was killing herself performing for a son who didn't think she was cute; yet the less he applauded, the harder she tried. As she explained to me, once she saw what she was doing and toned down her approach, her son began to respond to her. Now that he has grown up they understand each other. Without knowledge of the four personalities, we may wonder why we find people who see things our way only one time out of four. With this understanding, we can get along with people whether or not they are like us.

Ever the showman, the Sanguine parent would like to have the starring role and an eternal position on center stage without being responsible for any of the hard work or details. Responsibility is not a plus in this parent's mind, and frequently the other personalities call them airheads. However, mistakes that would embarrass others become fascinating material for the Sanguine's ever-growing reservoir of entertaining stories.

A lighthearted, possibly light-headed, Sanguine from Phoenix tells a story that would have been buried away in a box forever had it happened to a more serious person. For her nephew's sixth birthday she bought a darling tooth pillow for him to use after he pulled a tooth. She boxed it up, gift wrapped it, and mailed it to Tennessee, very proud of the "different" gift she had sent.

Later the boy's parents called and said there was nothing in the box; they wondered what had happened. Poor Aaron had looked and looked but found nothing. Our frazzled friend couldn't figure out what had happened; she even remembered putting the pillow in the box. Sure enough, back in the hall closet *in a box* was the pillow. Somehow she had mailed the wrong box. An empty one!

This kind of parent is most appreciated by children of a similar personality who can laugh along with them (not Melancholy kids who are often embarrassed by these parents!).

The Powerful Parent (**Choleric**)

Because the Powerful parent instantly becomes commander in chief in any situation, being in charge of the family seems a natural for her. All she has to do is line up the troops and give orders. It all sounds so simple. Cholerics believe that if everyone would only do things their way—immediately—we could all live happily ever after. The Choleric father is accustomed to giving firm orders in the business world without anyone second-guessing him, and he expects the same respect at home. A Choleric mother, often married to a Peaceful man who wouldn't dream of disagreeing with her, controls the family firmly, and her quick decisions are usually right. The home with Powerful parents is usually businesslike and fast paced—unless someone stages an insurrection.

Not only is such a home under control, but the Choleric parent is the one who can make work even out of leisure time. This individual doesn't like any rest and considers relaxing a sin to be avoided. One Powerful father took his children to Disneyland. He felt noble to be giving up his productive time to humor his family. He bought the tickets and let everyone know how much they cost. (The Powerful person seems unable to do anything without attaching a value to it. Every time my mother-in-law gave me a present she would say, "Be careful with that, it was very expensive.") This man marched his children into Disneyland for a "fun-filled" day. After an hour a cloudburst hit the area and his wife and children wanted to head for the car. "What do you think you're doing?" he asked. "We paid good money to get into this place and we are not going to let a little rain spoil our fun. You will go on the rides and you will enjoy them. We are going to get our money's worth!"

When this man's Peaceful wife told me the story, it was both pitiful and hilarious. "Can you imagine having fun on a roller coaster in pouring-down rain when you can't see a foot in front of you and the children are crying to go home?" she asked. This Powerful man not only got his money's worth, he also achieved another triumph. The family has never asked him to take them to Disneyland again!

A Powerful parent's strengths lie in motivational and action skills, while one of her weaknesses is an expectation of instant obedience from all those around. By learning to accept differences and by not just insisting on "your way," you can relax enough to tone down the tension your presence often brings into the home. Realize that three-fourths of the population don't have your drive, zest, stamina, and love for work, but that doesn't make them wrong, just different.

The Perfect Parent (Melancholy)

The Perfect parent is what all the others wish they were: clean, neat, organized, punctual, thoughtful, analytical, detail-conscious, compassionate, talented, dedicated, musical, patient, artistic, creative, poetic, sensitive, sincere, and steadfast. Could you ask for anything more? This parent takes on the raising of children as a serious lifetime project, and no other personality so totally dedicates itself to producing perfect children.

Often these parents resist using the four personalities as a tool because it seems too simple, seems to put unfair labels on people, and can't be found spelled out in Scripture. However, once they decide to give the idea a fair trial (since they are analytical people), they find its simplicity is able to explain complex issues. They learn the labels are needed to break personality down into understandable units, and the theory becomes a useful tool to obey the Bible's commands to examine ourselves; find our sins, failures, and weaknesses; and bring them before the Lord for forgiveness and cleansing.

Once Perfect people examine the use of the four personalities with an open mind, they become excited over how easily they can communicate this skill to their family and others. For the first time in her life, the deep Melancholy understands why other people don't all see things her way. Previously, she thought everyone should be a perfectionist like her and assumed everyone would want to be if they only knew how. Many have dedicated their lives to helping God conform others into what they perceived he wanted them to be. What an eye-opening experience to find only a fourth of the people in the world have the capacity or desire to do everything perfectly! Melancholy parents need to remember this or risk raising kids that don't fit a "perfect" mold despite their best efforts.

The Peaceful Parent (**Phlegmatic**)

Peaceful parents have the kind, low-key, relaxed, patient, sympathetic nature that we find so agreeable and acceptable in a father or mother. They don't argue or fight, they don't insist on high achievement, they roll with the punches, and they're never irrational or hysterical. What more could any child want? Many little ones would be glad to turn in their dramatic, emotional, Popular mother; their dictatorial, temperamental, Powerful father; or their critical, nit-picking Perfect parent for one Peaceful protector.

This easygoing parent has some shortcomings, though. Unless the Phlegmatic parent develops a set of guidelines for discipline and sticks to it, a Sanguine child may charm his way out of deserved consequences and a Choleric child will run the household. Peaceful parents must force themselves to invest energy into their relationships with their children, lest communication become nonexistent. The Phlegmatic parent who withdraws into her own world, retreating from the responsibility of being a parent, does no child any favors.

The greatest area of conflict and misunderstanding between parents and children seems to be with the opposite personality: Phlegmatic children can frustrate Choleric parents like no other; Melancholy children are most often misunderstood by Sanguine parents.

In part 2 of this book we will share real-life stories of interaction between all four personality types in children and their parents. To see where you fit into these scenarios, you must first identify your child's personality.

Listening Is the Answer

Your children will not have to be very old before you can sense their personalities. But you may wonder exactly how you can do this. JoAnn Hawthorn, teacher and school nurse, told me that she knows immediately what personality her little students are. "All the mothers need to do is first understand the personalities and then listen to their children. They will tell you who they are if you'll just listen to them."

Sunny Sanguines

Sanguine children are bright-eyed and engaging, and they use the word *fun* a lot. JoAnn told me about a three-year-old who turned around when leaving class and said, "Mrs. Hawthorn, Jack is *not* having any fun. We need to do something about it."

Popular Sanguine children like Jack will laugh a lot, love fun, and enjoy being with people. My daughter Marita was the life of the party from the time she was two years old.

Realize that your Sanguine children are inherently lighthearted, humorous, and energetic, with little ability to organize or remember instructions. The Sanguines' love of telling stories and wanting instant response often leads them into exaggerating the truth. They will get excited over every new project that comes along but will work only if they get enough praise for it. Oftentimes, they have little follow-through and will abandon one pursuit if a new one seems more fun.

Controlling Cholerics

Choleric children want their own way and think their ideas are better than those of the people in authority. A kindergartner informed JoAnn, "This is what I want to do today." When told that wasn't what JoAnn wanted to do, the child snapped back, "Well, it's what I want, so let's get started!"

The Powerful Choleric will give orders like these as soon as he can talk. Our little grandson Bryan, at twenty-one months, looked up at my husband one night, pointed in front of him with his finger, and stated clearly, "Poppa, here!" Fred moved immediately to his side, and Bryan knew he had Poppa under firm control.

If you have a Choleric child, he has probably already tried to take control of you and the rest of your children. Cholerics are born leaders, strong in every way, and usually right. They are out to win and will stop at nothing to achieve their end. Being a good worker is no problem for Cholerics as long as they feel appreciated. They will grab control if they sense a leadership vacuum or a power struggle between the parents. A Choleric child isn't intimidated just because we are bigger.

One lady told me she was trying to discipline her Choleric three-year-old. She told him to come downstairs, and he stood at the top and said, "No." She repeated her command three times and got the same response. Finally he put his pudgy little fists on his hips and replied, "Read my lips, NO!" Choleric children don't ever give in easily!

Meticulous Melancholies

Melancholy children are the teacher's dream. They like school, do their work quietly, and organize their equipment. When handed ten markers, a Melancholy child immediately counted them—twice—then sorted them according to color, lined them up perfectly, and announced, "Now I'm ready to start."

The Perfect Melancholy, who is well behaved and can be disciplined with just a disapproving glance, will start lining up his toys in rows when he is still a toddler. Our son Fred put all his stuffed animals in a certain order on his bed each day and if anyone moved one of them, he knew.

When you are dealing with a Melancholy child, you may constantly wonder why he is never happy. But Melancholies don't think they're unhappy; they just have a different level of pleasure. They don't like noise and confusion and prefer to be by themselves much of the time. These children will do projects perfectly as long as you recognize their ability and don't redo what has been accomplished. Let these children work alone if they desire; other people distract and frustrate them because they don't do anything right. These children make the best student and should be offered opportunities to pursue art, music, and drama. Melancholies usually have talent beyond the norm.

Pleasant Phlegmatics

Phlegmatic children are easy to get along with and will do whatever you ask most of the time. But they don't look for extra work, and underneath they have a stubborn will. If it happens to be one of their stubborn days, they don't want to change. One

Phlegmatic boy looked up at JoAnn and said simply, "I don't feel like doing this today." And he didn't.

Still, the Peaceful Phlegmatic is usually the child most eager to please. My son-in-law Randy, as a Phlegmatic child, went out with his parents many nights a week and sat quietly wherever they placed him, causing them no trouble.

If you have a Phlegmatic child, you have the easiest one to raise because he will want to stay out of trouble. He'll usually agree to do what you ask, but he'll test you to see if you mean business. If you forget to check on him or if you do the task yourself, that tells him that as long as he keeps the peace and looks willing, he won't be expected to do much work. This child has a dry sense of humor and is easily content.

By the time he is a teenager and you see that he has no goals or burning desire to achieve, you may begin to worry and ask yourself, *Where have we gone wrong?* I've learned that Phlegmatics are single-interest children, and our job is to locate that interest and help them develop it. My Phlegmatic son-in-law has always loved stamps and coins. He started as a boy, read books on what kings minted what coins, and started working in a coin store when he was in his early teens. Today he is president of that company, the Collector's Galleries in Redlands, California. Don't give up on these easygoing children! Find their interest and get them the equipment and lessons needed to reach their potential.

If you listen, you will understand what makes your children tick. Ask them how they feel about each other, about you, and about their teacher; then listen. Do they talk about fun? Tell you what to do? Aim for perfection? Or take it easy? They will tell you if you take the time to listen, and then you can meet their emotional needs, saving them from a life of searching for what they never got as a child.

God made all kinds of children and our purpose is to love them and accept them as they are and not try to make them over to be like us. Understanding and using the personality principles in this book will enable you to encourage each of your children differently according to his or her particular strengths, even if those don't conform to what you would have liked or expected.

We don't want cookie-cutter children who all say and do the same things. Instead, we want to see children free to function in their own unique version of their personality. By understanding their personalities, and hopefully our own too, we can more effectively parent them, give them an appreciation for who they are, and support them in the "way to go" they feel fits them best.

Putting It All Together

A young girl named Sue came to CLASS (Christian Leaders, Authors, and Speakers Seminar) and learned about the different personalities. She worked as a counselor in a home for underprivileged, abused, or orphaned children, and when she went back, she began to categorize her group. Since they had all come from dysfunctional families, they had lower motivation than would be expected of average children. The counselor decided to do some case studies, and she first divided them into four groups, according to their answers to some simple questions. One of her questions was, "If you could be any kind of person in the world, what or who would you choose to be?" Here are some of their answers:

Popular Sanguines wanted to be actors, comedians, TV stars in soap operas, cheerleaders, salespeople, Cinderella, or Miss Piggy.

Powerful Cholerics wanted to be kings and queens, president, Hitler, owners of big houses and limousines, highway patrol officers, and football players.

Perfect Melancholies dreamed of being musicians, artists, poets, bankers, Mozart in *Amadeus,* and Garfield the cat.

Peaceful Phlegmatics wanted to be rich so they didn't have to work, live on lakes with rowboats and canoes, be golf pros, have long vacations, and more recess.

As she worked with the groups, Sue found that the Populars were motivated by abundant praise, Powerfuls by appreciation of all their achievements, Perfects by her encouragement and observation of how well they had done each task, and the Peacefuls by a slow building of a trusting relationship in which they were finally convinced she valued them.

The other counselors were so impressed by the new and growing excitement in Sue's group that they asked her to teach them how to work with the personalities. One of the unexpected by-products of this division into groups according to their personalities was that this grouping gave insecure children an identity. For the first time in their lives they belonged to something positive; they became real people.

As I have counseled depressed teenagers, one of their consistent complaints is "I'm a nobody." They don't know who they are and they are sure their parents know even less about them. This lack of identity and self-worth is what propels some of them into cults where they are warmly welcomed and made to feel part of a group.

How great it would be if we could help all of our children understand who they are and that we accept them exactly as they are, not as we wish they would turn out to be. Understanding your personality and that of your child will enable you as a parent to help your child develop his or her strengths and overcome weaknesses to become a capable, confident individual who is ready to face the future.

PART 2

Living with the Personalities

three

SIGNS OF A SUNNY SANGUINE

SANGUINE

Popular Personality
The Extrovert • The Talker • The Optimist

Emotional Needs: attention, approval, affection, acceptance, presence of people and activity

Avoids: dull tasks, routines, criticism, details, lofty goals

Strengths	Weaknesses
BABY	
• bright and wide-eyed • curious • gurgles and coos • wants company • shows off • responsive	• screams for attention • knows she is cute • grabby, into everything • cries when no one picks her up or when tired

Strengths	Weaknesses
CHILD	
• daring and eager	• no follow-through
• innocent	• disorganized
• inventive and imaginative	• easily distracted
• cheerful	• short interest span
• enthusiastic	• emotional ups and downs
• fun-loving	• wants credit
• chatters constantly	• tells fibs
• bounces back	• forgetful
• energized by people	
TEEN	
• cheerleader	• deceptive
• charms others	• creative excuses
• gets daring	• easily led astray
• joins clubs	• craves attention
• popular	• needs peer approval
• life of the party	• con artist
• creative	• won't study
• wants to please	• immature
• apologetic	• gossips

Blue-eyed, dark-haired two-year-old Heather, while in a McDonald's fast-food restaurant, got bored with her Happy Meal, stood up, turned around to face the rest of the people eating, put her arms in the air as if to embrace them all, and said in a voice that needed no microphone, *"Hi everybody!"*

Popular Sanguines have an innate desire for fun and games from the time they are little. Their cheerful inquisitiveness endears them to others, and they are happy as long as they can laugh and be loved by the people around them. A perpetual twinkle in their eyes, these creative children will delight (or exasperate) adults with their antics. Sanguines always seem to have more fun than those around them, so others flock to be around them. The enjoyment of the attention they receive from others represents their first great emotional need.

The Four A's

From birth Sanguines love people and desire *attention.* Sanguine babies want to move from room to room with you and will often cry if left alone. As young children and teens they need you to look them in the eye and listen to them. They see life as a production where they are the stars, and they want their audience to listen and respond. Life runs more smoothly for both you and your child when you sit down and listen for a period of time instead of putting her off with, "Not now, later."

The Sanguine's second great need is *approval.* Without notice and praise for every little thing she accomplishes, the Sanguine child will give up trying to please. For these children, being criticized or ignored is like having water poured over creative flames. They want their every thought and action to be a "big deal" with you. But you don't need to worry that their heads will swell at the praise. I've talked to many teens who were in despair, and none of them attributed their depression to being praised too much.

Of all types, Sanguines are the most needy for touchy-feely *affection.* To them love is hugs, kisses, and holding hands. Of course, when they become teens, they will prefer you don't embrace them too much in public, but they do need constant affirmation of your love.

Sanguines need your *acceptance* of them as they are, not as they might become someday if they work hard enough to please you. If they grow up with high-achieving siblings who get most of your praise and acceptance, these children are left with the feeling that until they become like their siblings, they will not be good enough for their parents. When Sanguines don't feel accepted by their parents, they try to find someone else who will take them as they are. This quest can lead them into unhealthy relationships.

Sanguine Suzie's parents are professional people with a combined above-average income and she has her own well-decorated room in a large house. On the surface we see that she lives in the lap of luxury, but her parents are so busy that they have little time for her. She's well cared for by sitters, but Suzy is desperate for her *parents'* attention. They don't have time to sit down and listen to her endless stories and when they do talk with Suzie, they tell her how to do her chores better. Dinnertime has become a correction session that discourages Suzie, and criticism without any words of approval has caused her to lose interest in doing anything right.

Suzie wishes her father would notice her, put his arms around her, and really hug her more often. One day she asked him if he loved her, and he answered, "Of course; why do you think we had you if we didn't want you?" This businesslike reply didn't help Suzie very much. She wanted an assurance of her father's affection. Instead, she was left to doubt and wonder, "Do my parents wish they had a different child? They don't have time for me; nothing I do is right." Based on her perceptions that her parents don't seem to love her, Suzie has concluded, "I don't think they really like me as I am."

Suzie's conclusion hasn't helped her poor personal relationships in school. Teachers are irritated by her constant talking and the way she hangs on them for attention. She has become the class clown to make others laugh, but they laugh at her rather than with her. In her desire for someone to love her, she has begun to mix with the wrong crowd because they seem to accept her as she is.

Is Suzie doomed because her parents are extremely busy? Not necessarily, but parents with Sanguine children shouldn't take such a chance by neglecting their kids. Spend quality time giving these children meaningful affection and let them know they are accepted for who they are. For Sanguines, *attention, approval, affection, and acceptance* are the food of life, and they're always hungry. Don't forget to feed them!

Sanguine Charm

Sanguines can charm their parents into things that their siblings could never get away with. Brie-Anne was trying to negotiate getting a brand-new colorful binder for her science fair project. She didn't really need a new binder; she had one that would work very well. But it would be much more fun to shop for a new one with a pretty design or even a holographic cover. She and her mother discussed this possible purchase as Brie-Anne was getting into bed. Her mother decided she wasn't going to commit to buying a new binder. Then came Brie-Anne's prayer that night: "Thank you, God, that Mom is going to take me tomorrow to get a new binder." Brie-Anne went on with the rest of her prayer, praising her mom. As her mother started praying that Brie-Anne would sleep well, the child jumped in, "We interrupt this prayer to thank you that Mom is going to take me to buy a new binder tomorrow." You guessed it—Brie-Anne ended up with a very colorful *new* binder for her project.

The Sanguine's charm is hard to resist! As parents, we need to mean what we say, or these wily children will learn quite early in life that "no" only means "Ask again nicer, and if possible put God on your side."

Answer for Everything

It's hard to ever outwit Sanguines as they have an answer for everything and think they are funny. When others don't appreciate their humor, they try even harder. Outgoing Sanguine Sally took our personality test and checked off everything she would like to be. Her skeptical Melancholy husband reviewed her scores and claimed the test couldn't be accurate because Sally's scores totaled more than 100 percent. Sally, however, charmed him into taking the test himself. He complained again when he discovered that his numbers totaled somewhat less than 100. "It's simple dear," Sally explained. "I've just got more personality than you!" She went off happy that she had come up with such a good line, and he was depressed for days.

You can help your Sanguine child refrain from impulsive, glib remarks that might offend or depress someone else. Encourage her sense of humor and praise her for her wit, but teach her to understand that if she doesn't stop to think first, her words can wound others.

Need to Fill Gaps

Sanguines love to talk and often aren't comfortable with silence. Brie-Anne knows she has a tendency to fill up dead space with conversation, especially in situations where she may feel somewhat nervous or self-conscious. She has been praying before she enters one of these situations that the Lord would help her to not talk so much and to resist the urge to fill up the dead spaces. What a difference that has made for her! She can see already at thirteen that her friends like her better when she doesn't monopolize all the conversation.

Help your child realize what Brie-Anne has learned. Teach her that others will appreciate her more if she allows others to talk instead of always filling the gaps herself. Sanguines love to talk and feel what they have to say is more interesting than what others are saying. So it's especially important for you to teach them not to always jump in with comments of their own but to let others have a chance to speak.

Adventures

Sanguines can make an adventure out of almost anything. What is a list of chores to most people becomes a day of excitement for a Sanguine. My mother often sighed, "I've never seen anyone like you. You could go into a store for a loaf of bread and come out with enough material to write a book!" Little did she know, I really could!

From the time I was a child I could make a story out of anything. The people who came into our family's store all became characters on the live stage of my imagination. I was never bored—each time the door opened and a new person entered, I began a new scene in my mind. I taught my young brothers how to pantomime the customers, and on dull days we amused ourselves with our own brand of charades. It was my observations of the ever-changing cast we had before us that gave me material for my early writing.

Recently I found a box full of my grammar school papers. I was fascinated at all the adventures I had written about. For a child who never went anywhere, I had a very colorful life!

Spills

Sanguine children are so emotional and impulsive that they often trip, drop, or spill. A young family stopped at McDonald's for breakfast on their way to Big Bear. Because they were in a hurry, they went to the drive-thru. As the children started eating in the car, the mother leaned over to the youngest son, a Sanguine who was about eight years old at the time, and said, "Try not to spill the syrup on your clothes." Without missing a beat, he said, "Mom, when was the last time I *tried* to spill food on myself?"

Sanguine children don't try to make a mess. They just aren't naturally neat like their Melancholy siblings. Accept their scattered attention span and don't make them feel they are peculiar.

Instead, help them learn to cope with their clumsy tendencies rather than scream when they dump a glass of milk in your lap.

What's in a Name?

Sanguines have difficulty remembering names for two reasons: they don't listen when they first hear a name and they don't care. These kids believe they are so adorable that you will overlook a mistake so minor as not remembering your name. Five-year-old Trent met a new neighbor named Trevor. While running to base playing kick-the-can, Trent called out, "Come on, Joseph!" When Trent's mother pointed out that his friend's name was really Trevor, Trent replied, "That's all right, Mom. He said I could call him Joseph."

Try helping your Sanguine child associate names with something colorful or funny or with something that rhymes. Names aren't the most important things for your child to remember, but learning to do so will improve their relationships with others in the future.

Sanguine Spending

Sanguines measure things by how much fun they're having, regardless of the cost. This perspective will especially frustrate Melancholy parents or siblings. Beverly and her two Sanguine daughters told me about their bread-making machine. They had a lot of fun with it, and the bread was getting better with each batch. As they gushed about this mechanical wonder and their ability to use it, Beverly's Melancholy husband looked at his wife and daughters and said with a sigh, "It's now down to only five dollars a loaf."

Although Sanguines don't want to be reminded of the cost of fun, parents do need to teach their children a measure of financial responsibility. Give them limits on how much they can spend and let them decide what to buy. Sanguines won't take to bookkeeping like their Melancholy siblings, but they can learn to keep themselves from going broke.

Obsessed with Clothes

Sanguine girls and boys love clothes from a very early age and can become obsessed with their looks. They like bright colors and the latest fads because they draw the attention they always seek. Five-year-old Sanguine Trent bypassed the clothes his mother had picked out for him to wear to school. Instead, he grabbed a wild red shirt with big flowers. His grandmother had bought him the shirt while on a trip to Hawaii. His mother thought it was "too much" for him to wear to school. But he wouldn't let her take it off, and now he wants to wear it every day. He thinks he is one hot ticket—and he is!

Four-year-old Popular Brooklynn showers her older brother Bryan with sweet butterfly kisses and adoring words. Thirteen-year-old Melancholy Bryan is your typical junior high student who worries a lot about the opinion of his peers, so he loves her attention at home but not in front of his friends.

One day when Beth told Brooklynn that it was time to pick Bryan up from school, the four-year-old responded, "Oh! What is he wearing?" As Brooklynn raced to the dress-up drawer, Beth hollered for her to hurry and heard, "I need a hat!"

It was tough for Beth to keep a straight face as Brooklynn traipsed to the door. She had decorated her navy, floor-length men's suit jacket with a tiger tail left over from another costume. A pair of old flight glasses rested crooked on her nose, and a metallic gold-and-red hat trimmed in black velvet crowned her little head. Her accessories were second to none—white gloves covered her hands and a strappy stiletto shoe served as her purse. "Do I look like Bryan?" she wondered out loud.

The pair drove up to the school, where a hundred or so junior high students were milling in the parking lot. Beth honked and waved at Bryan. The smile on his face faded as he approached the car. His darling sister was hanging out the window in her garish outfit, waving frantically and calling his name, "Bryan, Bryan, over here!"

Barely in the car, Bryan yelled, "GO! GO! GO!" Shrinking low and pulling his cap over his eyes, he took command of the speedy exit. To his credit, once the school was out of sight, he did compliment Brooklynn on her taste in clothing. She sweetly replied, "I look just like you!"

Mothers of young children must recognize that clothes are fun and should not be too concerned about the wild combinations their little ones create. If you let your Sanguine children have fun with clothes when they're little, they're less apt to rebel with weird outfits as teens.

Modesty

Sanguine girls can learn early the value of sex appeal in getting attention. Barb's Sanguine daughter Alethea loves attention. When it came time for her junior prom, she came out to the living room to show her mother the new dress she'd bought. Barb's jaw dropped to the floor when she saw Alethea's more than ample bosom pouring out of the black velvet bodice. "You are *not* going to the prom looking like that!" she exclaimed. Barb wanted to get a piece of black velvet and sew it on the dress all the way up to her daughter's chin, but she remembered how important it was to Alethea that she receive admiration and attention. Mother and daughter had a long talk about modesty, and Barb ended up sewing a smaller piece of matching fabric to her dress that still showed a little of her beautiful figure.

It's up to parents to teach their Sanguine child modesty while still allowing her to be the belle of the ball. If you have a Sanguine child who uses his or her sexuality to grab attention or admiration, teach your child the value of dressing modestly. Don't respond too rigidly, however, or he or she may rebel and dress even more provocatively . . . away from home.

Unusual Creativity

Sanguine children come up with very creative, offbeat ways of doing things. Sanguine Will's mother told me about an oral book report Will had to prepare for his class. He was to dress as a character and give his report. He chose Ribsy from Beverly Cleary's *Henry and Ribsy.* The Sunday evening before he was to give the report, his mother asked him what he was going to say. He stood in front of her and said, "Ruff, ruff, ruff, ruff, ruff. In doggy talk that means, 'Hi! I'm Ribsy.'" Then he proceeded to give a five-minute report on *Henry and Ribsy*—and every other Beverly Cleary book that Ribsy is in! It was great! On the day of the report, every other child stood up and read reports that declared, "The character I chose was . . . the book I read was . . ." Will did his report just as he had practiced, and the whole class, the parents, and his teacher *loved* it. He was the hit of the day!

Make sure when your Sanguine child becomes unusually creative that you don't stifle her imagination in an effort to make her conform to the ordinary in life. Instead, encourage your child to use her unusual imagination.

Colorful Perspectives

Creative Sanguine children see things in pictures and use expressions others wouldn't always choose. When Marita was in kindergarten, her teacher sent me a note expressing concern that Marita had done a drawing of her mother that portrayed me with purple hair. I asked Marita what made her decide to draw me with purple hair. She quickly answered, "They didn't have any blond crayons."

Ten-year-old Peter wanted to make a special birthday card for his ninety-seven-year-old great grandpa, a former golfer. With no coaching from anyone, he wrote, "Grandpa Mac, your life has been a ninety-seven-yard line drive and you have about a three-foot putt left."

Encourage your child's ability to make life colorful and don't try to put her in a dull gray mold. The Sanguine's colorful creativity brings life to dreary days!

four

PARENTING YOUR SANGUINE CHILD

If you're the parent of a Sanguine child, you're in for a treat. Life will be exciting with this bundle of energy around, but you'll need to teach him to balance fun with focus and discipline.

Because they're easily distracted, Sanguine children need constant supervision to see that they do what they were assigned. At times you may feel it would be easier to do the task yourself, but that only teaches children that doing a chore poorly will prevent them from being asked to do it again. Instead, make sure you praise your child for anything he *does* accomplish. Remember that Sanguines thrive on approval, and if they are complimented for achieving a small task today, they may do more tomorrow.

Sanguines are notorious for speaking before thinking, so you'll need to teach your child to be careful about what he says. You'll never completely succeed in keeping thoughtless remarks from flying off a Sanguine's tongue, but you can help him realize what he's doing.

Despite the difficulty they have completing assigned tasks, Sanguines frequently commit themselves to multiple projects. Recognizing their enthusiasm for new, exciting activities and their inability to say *no* to anyone, help your Sanguine children evaluate their schedules realistically. Compliment their charisma and help them decline a few opportunities to be center stage, but don't cut off all their outside activities.

Regardless of your personality as a parent, you'll find that you must allow your Sanguine child to have fun but teach him that goals and discipline are necessary for success. Depending on your own personality, however, there are specific considerations you'll need to understand.

Popular Parent with a Popular Child

Popular Sanguine children and parents share a zest for life and a sense of humor that bind them together. They possess natural optimism and enthusiasm for life as well as a natural ability to compliment each other profusely. Marita and I have what we call our mutual admiration society. Anytime we need a pick-me-up, we call each other. There are some pitfalls to this combination, but few Sanguines really care.

Your Attention, Please

Because both of them enjoy being in the spotlight, Sanguine parents and children may find themselves competing for center stage. Popular parents must be careful to avoid such competition, especially during a child's teenage years. When a teenage Sanguine girl brings home a boyfriend, her mother may be tempted to divert the boy's attention to herself. If the daughter complains, the Popular parent, always wide-eyed and innocent, typically responds, "What did I do wrong? I was only being pleasant to your friend." Sanguine parents need to beware of such conflicts or all the mutual love and admiration these two share will be replaced by competitive jealousy.

Plans without Action

In their pursuit of happiness Popular Sanguines may never get life pulled together. Sanguine students are frequently voted Miss Congeniality or Most Likely to Succeed. But unless they are forced to set goals and get organized, they may miss their potential mark. Emilie Barnes told me of a friend she tried to help with her speaking. "She has so much talent and a magnetic personality," said Emilie. "She could have been a great success, but I couldn't get her to focus on one area and do it well. As soon as she got going, she'd get bored and try something else. So, unfortunately, today she's right where she was when I started with her years ago." To avoid such disappointment, Sanguine parents must make an extra effort to instill a sense of discipline in their Sanguine children.

Sanguine parents with Sanguine children must find some focus and touch of organization themselves, then show their children that such qualities are needed to reach their maximum potential. A scattered Sanguine sows seeds of possibility; but with no sense of focus for the future, the seeds seldom bear fruit.

Discipline Is Fun

Little Sanguine children are able to convince their friends that whatever punishment they are receiving is really fun. Jo-Anne shared with me an example of this from her young life. Jo-Anne's mother didn't know how to handle Jo-Anne with her high energy. In an attempt to bridle her energy and outgoing nature, her desperate mother tied her to a tree in the front lawn. She hoped that this would humiliate the four-year-old enough that Jo-Anne would stay put and behave like her Melancholy sister. Instead, Jo-Anne managed to convince all the neighbors' kids that this was a wonderful thing and they all begged their parents to tie them to their trees!

Phony Repentance

As a child, my daughter Marita alternated between making discipline appear fun and wailing loudly over the thought of a spanking. A couple of years ago at the Christian Booksellers Association convention, a little Sanguine girl came to our booth. She was a replica of Marita at the age of five. When Marita asked the girl what she wanted to be when she grew up, she said, "I will be a comedian." Her mother interrupted and stated, "God has a call on her life, and she will be a Christian singer." As her mother went on to explain "the call," the child put her fingers in her ears, shook her head, and sang loudly. Her mother was furious and muttered, "I don't know what to do with her." As the mother turned away, the child said to Marita, "I really get to her and I'm always in a lot of trouble." Marita responded to the girl with tips on how to avoid painful punishment: "When you see her coming, start to cry, and when she spanks you, start wailing immediately so she thinks you're hurt. Once you convince her that you are in pain and that you're sorry, she will stop spanking you. All parents really want out of you is a spirit of repentance. I'm sure you'll learn how to be convincing with a little practice." As I heard Marita teaching phony repentance, I realized that was what she'd done with me and I had believed her.

Everyone Loves Me

Sanguines delight in being loved. One Sanguine grandmother told me she has the most fun with her Sanguine granddaughter Aimee because they think so much alike. One day while playing together in the pool, Grandma grabbed Aimee and said, "I really love you, honey." With Sanguine self-assurance Aimee replied, "I know. You love me; Mommy loves me;

Daddy loves me; Jesus loves me. *Everyone I've ever met loves me!*"

When your Sanguine child has her love tank filled, she'll travel through life fueled by joy and able to bring sparkles of love to others along the journey.

Powerful Parent with a Popular Child

The Powerful Choleric parent with the fun-loving Popular Sanguine child can be an excellent combination. They share an optimistic outlook and enjoyment of people, and their cheerful attitude toward accomplishments makes them a great team. One gets the work done while the other entertains.

Parents must be careful, however, not to minimize the difference between the two personalities. The weaknesses of this combination become apparent when parents don't understand their own personalities. Because Powerful parents love work and quick results, they think everyone should be working like them.

When Can We Rest?

Carried to an extreme a Powerful parent's compulsion for work (and expectation that others keep up) can overwhelm the Popular child. Such a child will likely decide to stay out of the parent's path and find somewhere else to have fun. As a mother, I approached work in a Choleric manner—and I expected the same from my children. One day Lauren said to me, "If I ever wanted to rest I sure wouldn't come home." If your Sanguine child spends more time with the lady down the street than with you, perhaps he perceives you as a drill sergeant and knows that going home means having to work—and that's no fun!

Lots of Love

Sanguine children look for love wherever they can find it. The Choleric parent who understands this emotional need can win her child's undying affection by clearly expressing what is expected behavior and then offering lavish praise when performance comes anywhere close to the set standards. Sanguine children are motivated by compliments and approval and are devastated by criticism. Appreciate their humor, don't make fun of them, and give them plenty of affection. Your child will gladly follow your leadership as long as you offer plenty of praise.

Adorable Antics

Sometimes the Popular child with his winning ways becomes the pet of the Powerful parent and is able to con the parent and get away with behavior for which the others would be punished. I can remember Marita as a child taking money from my wallet and buying me a geranium with *my* money. I thought she was cute and adorable and for a while I didn't even see it as a negative action. How can you get angry with a child who steals money from you and then buys you a present with what she stole?

Remember, though, that your Popular child loves to act and knows how to become what he perceives you want. Acting is fun, especially if it produces results!

That's No Fun!

While unemotional, task-oriented Cholerics are focused on results, Sanguines are passionate about making every situation in life fun. Little Sanguine Anne loves attention and she gets it from her Choleric grandfather who dotes on her. She loves it when he mentions her in his sermons and brings her presence to the attention of the congregation. When her grandfather was asked to be the guest preacher at a local church, Anne kept asking him if he was going to mention her from the pulpit. About a day or so before her grandfather was going to preach, Anne asked him, "Grandpa, what's the title of your sermon?" He said, "When Heaven Is Silent." Somewhat disappointed, never-silent Anne said, "Well, how are you going to fit me into a sermon on that?"

Another time when she asked him what he was going to preach on, he told her the sermon was going to be about hell. Anne said, "Well, that's depressing. Why don't you talk about me because then it would be fun and wouldn't be depressing at all!"

If Choleric parents are willing to listen, they'll find the young Sanguine's penchant for fun refreshing. And the children might just interject a new zest for life into their practical parents!

Perfect Parent with a Popular Child

Perfect Melancholy parents with Popular Sanguine children can be an exciting blend of opposite personalities that fills in each other's empty spaces. Perfect parents can help their children develop much-needed organizational skills, while Sanguine children can interject humor and fun into the home. It's not easy to produce a balanced blend, however. In fact, without understanding the personalities, these two tend to bring out the worst in each other and are the most volatile combination.

Aren't You Done Yet?

Melancholy parents who expect each child to do things on time and correctly discover that their Sanguine child doesn't have a serious thought or an organized mind. Whereas you are naturally organized and disciplined, your child is not. So you need to help your young Sanguine learn to develop the discipline that you've mastered. Be careful, though, not to constantly criticize your child. That won't get you anywhere.

When the Sanguine child doesn't get the praise he so desperately needs, the child's will to perform disappears. Critical and nit-picking parents make these children feel hopeless, and they shut down their bubbling personalities, saving their humor for people who appreciate them. Without an appreciative audience at home, the Sanguine child feels worthless and his need for approval may motivate him to become the class clown or a discipline problem. The Sanguine child will get attention in any way possible—positive or negative.

To avoid this problem, focus on the positive with your child, rewarding jobs well done with praise and opportunities for creative fun. Motivate your child to stay focused by giving him the love and approval he needs when he's tried to please you.

Neat and Clean? No Way!

Sanguines love to work or clean house when it's fun, but don't expect the tasks to be completed perfectly. Melancholy Eva Marie was frustrated with her Sanguine daughter right from the beginning. She tried desperately to teach her to get organized, to pick up after herself, and to do all the tasks so dear to the Melancholy's heart. "You'll never amount to anything if you don't get your life in order," Eva Marie repeatedly told her daughter, sincerely believing the melancholy statements she steadily dropped on Jessica's head. Jessica learned to ignore her mother's instructions and move on happily in her Sanguine way.

Eva Marie reports that years of gentle guidance and screaming temper tantrums have resulted in an eighteen-year-old-girl-woman-slob who is lovely to look at with her wide smile and dancing blue eyes. Her hair is neatly groomed. Her makeup looks as though it were professionally applied. She appeals to everyone she meets. She walks into a room and all eyes go to her. If she lived in a hole, she'd be popular with the moles and gophers. But that hasn't changed her habits at home. Eva Marie has learned to enjoy her daughter's personality rather than complaining about Jessica's room. And Jessica likes her mom a whole lot more because of that.

Realize that no matter how hard you try, your Sanguine children will never be neat and clean enough to match your perfect standards. Learn to compromise by allowing some messiness in designated areas. At least you'll be able to control the mess that way. Remember, bedrooms have doors; shut them and walk away!

What Checklist?

Melancholy parents tend to base discipline on "normal" behavior. The parent sets down the rules and puts up a chart; the children follow the rules and check off the chart. It sounds simple. But for the Sanguine child—who forgets what he's doing while traveling from one room to the next, lives only for the moment and can't see long-range consequences (he performs even menial tasks for the praise of an audience)—the thought of making a bed alone in his room and then remembering to put a check on a chart borders on the impossible.

Follow the Leader

If you are a Perfect parent who expects all your children to line up behind you like little ducks following the leader, you'll save yourself numerous migraine headaches if you can see your Sanguine child as a God-given court jester, presented to you for comic relief in a heavy world. Realize that he is probably not going to be a nuclear physicist, but be confident that your child's charm and ability to tell a story better than anyone else will take him places you never dreamed possible.

My mother wanted all of her children to be musicians, so she signed each of us up for music lessons. With some effort I learned to play a few hymns on the piano, Jim took piano and singing lessons, and Ron played the trumpet well enough to be in the high school band. But our Popular personalities were more interested in being funny than in practicing notes.

When Ron was still in grammar school, he began to memorize lyrics from Spike Jones records. He was able to lip-synch them perfectly and he collected sound-effects items to enhance his performance. He found an old galvanized tub and spent days filling a pail with broken glass. At a certain point in one record he would pour the glass chunks from the pail into the tub, making a horrendous racket. Each time he did this, my mother screamed and grabbed a door frame for support, convinced the world was coming to an end. She tried to dissuade him from his "tomfool pranks," but he happily persisted. During high school Ron was in shows, wrote singing commercials, and became a disc jockey—all instead of doing his homework. Mother was sure he'd never amount to a "row of pins," but today he is the most popular radio personality in the Dallas/Fort Worth area and has made more money by being funny than Mother could have ever imagined.

My brother Jim became a career chaplain in the Air Force and retired as a full colonel. I taught English and speech and now write and speak. We have all made our livings with our mouths in spite of our mother's hand-wringing and pessimistic prophecies. Our "talking too much" has paid off!

Realize that not every child is going to do "normal" things. Then encourage each child according to his or her particular strengths, even if he or she doesn't conform to what you would have liked or expected. Don't keep saying, "Why can't you be more like so-and-so." And don't try to jam square pegs into round holes.

Brace Yourself for the Whirlwind

While a Melancholy parent thrives on peace and quiet order, Sanguine children frequently look for excitement, energy, and noise. Recently, during a two-week house-sitting job, Jessica stopped home to have dinner with her parents. Eva Marie described how invitingly neat and quiet the house had been before her daughter's arrival—with the exception of a purring cat, there wasn't a single sound to distract her from the novel she was reading. Then Jessica arrived. The door to the garage slammed shut. "It's so dark in here!" she exclaimed. Every light came on in her path. "What are you doing? Why is it so quiet? It's too quiet!" She fired rapid questions as she entered the sanctuary of the living room and briskly picked up the remote control for the television. The room was immediately filled with the sounds of a Tarzan movie—elephants, apes, and other indistinguishable sounds from the jungle. "It was peaceful," Eva Marie remarked, only to have Jessica smile brightly and reply, "It was depressing!"

Sanguines and Melancholies will probably never see eye to eye on what constitutes a "perfect" environment, but by understanding each other's personalities, you can learn to live together peacefully.

You Don't Understand!

Sanguines want others to get emotional with them and feel their pain. As parents we can't make snap judgments without taking some of our precious time to commiserate with understanding and true feeling. In her book *Staying Friends with Your Kids,* Kathy Collar Miller tells about how she learned this lesson.[3] Kathy learned how to deal with her Sanguine child even though she didn't have a personal feeling for her emotions.

When her daughter Darcy was in elementary school, Kathy walked by her bedroom and heard her crying. Kathy opened the door and peeked in to see Darcy sitting on her bed, tears spilling down her cheeks. "What happened?" Kathy asked, imagining some horrible thing.

Darcy looked up at her mother with a quivering lip and cried out, "I don't have anyone to play with." Relief and disbelief began rising in Kathy—how ridiculous that this should cause such a fuss, she thought. Fortunately Kathy understood Darcy's Sanguine love for people and her need to constantly be having fun with others. By reminding herself of that, Kathy was able to sympathize with her and understand the reason for her tears.

Still, it's not quite that simple, as Kathy found out. As a Melancholy, Kathy frequently tried to repeat the feelings her Sanguine daughter was having without getting emotional herself. But as time went on this practice only made Darcy more upset. She sensed that her mother's verbal concerns were an act. While Kathy was stating that she understood her daughter's dramatic depression, her lack of passion about those emotions communicated that she didn't really care. Although it's difficult for Melancholy parents to let the emotions loose, they must do so or they'll never convince their kids that they really do understand.

No Place like Home . . . Except . . .

While Sanguine children usually love the warm, homey atmosphere a Melancholy mom can create, they still have the need to go out into the world and socialize. Melancholy Barb prided herself on a clean home, with lots of good books, videos, and fun activities for her children. Since she had read countless parenting books and created a house filled with love and warmth, Barb felt rejected when her Sanguine daughter, Alethea, went elsewhere seeking fun.

From the time Alethea was about three years old, while her brother and sister were playing a game or reading, Alethea would leave. Barb would panic and walk around the neighborhood before finding Alethea at a neighbor's house watching them garden or helping bake cookies. Everyone adored Alethea and they were happy to have her. But Barb wondered what was so lacking in her home that Alethea had to go to someone else's to find fun. When she learned about the personalities, Barb realized that Sanguines gather up as much love and attention as they can, always seeking a new stage for their continual performances. For Sanguine Alethea that stage was frequently found out the front door.

Melancholy parents of Sanguine children need to give their kids permission to go out and be more social than they might want to be themselves. Don't worry, your Sanguine will be back . . . after the last act of the day.

Too Much Detail

Melancholy parents are great at remembering and describing every little detail, but kids don't always need to hear it. Sanguine Charlie was twelve years old when he went to his Melancholy mom to find out what the word *rigmarole* meant. Charlie had been with the neighbor children whose mother had used this word, and they didn't understand what she meant. Charlie ran into the house to get a quick answer so he could run back outside and tell his friends. Afraid that his mom might say, "Go look it up in the dictionary," Charlie was happy when she started to explain the word to him. But five minutes later Mom was still explaining the Latin roots of the word, and Charlie was getting antsy. His mother sensed his lack of interest and talked even more to get her son to pay attention. The more she insisted, the more he resisted. Finally, she decided that he should go get the book *Little Women* (only a Melancholy could remember this book uses the word *rigmarole* in it) and spend the rest of his afternoon reading. Every night for two weeks Charlie had to read the book. "My friends felt sorry for me," recalls Charlie, now an adult. "Everyone in the neighborhood made fun of my mom and called her Mrs. Lecture. I hated that book and I hated Mom for making me read it. All I did was ask her one simple question, and she turned it into a two-week study. After that I made sure I never asked her advice or opinion on anything."

Melancholy parents should be careful not to force their interests on their children or to insist that they understand more than is necessary for their age or the question. As the old saying goes, "When you want to know what time it is, you don't need to hear how to build a clock."

The Moral of the Story

Melancholies also have a tendency to turn every Sanguine story into a morality play. A child may relate a humorous account of the crazy thing he did today, and the parent points out how to never make that mistake again. After a while the child stops talking at all at home and saves his humor for his friends.

I have often talked with Sanguine teens whose parents think they are Melancholy. When I ask the teen how this is possible, they say their parents don't think their stories are funny and whatever they do tell them gets corrected or rejected so they just don't tell them anything anymore. They shut themselves in their room and save their real personality for their friends. We parents need to learn to listen, not interrupt, and not make every Sanguine story into the impetus for a moral lecture. Enjoy your Sanguine teens and laugh with them or you will become one of those parents who say to me, "How can I get him to talk?"

Why Don't My Kids Love Me like That?

Sometimes Sanguine children bond more deeply with other Sanguines than they do with their own parents. Melancholy parents often have a hard time expressing physical affection, sometimes withholding it until the child has performed to certain standards. When a Melancholy parent gives sparingly in the area of touch, Sanguines will seek hugs and kisses wherever they can find them.

Melancholy Debbie shared the story of her Sanguine sister-in-law's visit. Debbie's son had met Aunt Rose when he was four years old, but his sisters didn't know her at all. They loved her! She played with them, sang songs, taught them piano duets and magic tricks. Debbie's youngest daughter, Carolyn, the only Sanguine in the family, grew very attached to Aunt Rose and physically hung on her the whole time. In the mornings she crawled into bed with her and the day Aunt Rose left, Carolyn would not let go of her. When Rose went home, Carolyn bawled her eyes out. Debbie knows Carolyn loves her but she actually felt a little jealous of the attention Carolyn gave Rose and of the obvious emotional bonding that took place so quickly. They were "two peas in a pod."

Whether it's a visitor, teacher, friend, or relative, Sanguine children will bond with the first Sanguine that comes in the door. If you're a Melancholy parent, make sure you are giving your Sanguine children *time, attention,* and *physical touch,* or they'll find someone else who will!

Peaceful Parent with a Popular Child

Sanguine children bring out the humorous side of their Phlegmatic parents. These parents love to have a good time as long as someone else is preparing the party; and the Popular child loves to instigate parties as long as someone will come. Sanguines are a constant source of entertainment and they thrive on the response they receive from these Peaceful parents. Despite their ability to enjoy a good time together, however, this pair will encounter a few problems.

Road to Accomplishment

Since neither parent nor child possesses natural organizational skills, this pair is the least apt to get anything accomplished that isn't downright fun. Neither one is very responsible, and they both hope someone else will show up to do the work. Phlegmatic parents must work to develop organizational skills so they can model them for their children. Without a little organization and responsibility, these children will have many friends but few accomplishments.

All's Well When It's Quiet

Sanguine children love Phlegmatic parents because they can do what they want and, as long as they don't make noise, they don't get in trouble. Cindy told us about her Phlegmatic husband and an afternoon with their Sanguine and Choleric children. Cindy wanted to go shopping and asked Phlegmatic Don if he could manage their creative six-year-old Sanguine, their controlling four-year-old Choleric, and her four-year-old friend. In typical Phlegmatic fashion, Don agreed, "No problem. Glad to do it."

Don decided to take a shower in the middle of the afternoon, and while he was doing so, his six-year-old came to the shower, banged on the door, opened it a crack, and handed him two new cans of spray paint, requesting, "We can't get the tops off. Would you help us?" Being an obliging father, Don took the caps off and gave the cans back.

By the time Cindy came home, the girls had spray-painted the basement in stripes of pink and green and were a little too colorful themselves. Once she finished screaming in shock, Cindy questioned her husband: "How did they get the paint? Where were you?" She couldn't believe that he had opened the cans. When asked why he had done so, Don replied, "Because they asked me to." And as long as the kids were quiet and seemed happy, it didn't occur to him to check on them.

Your Attention, Please!

Sanguine children can act silly, goofy, or even outrageous, hamming it up while a Peaceful Phlegmatic parent stays calm and takes their antics in stride. However, the laid-back approach to parenting can backfire with a Sanguine who needs a parent's attention. Five-year-old Rose had been in kindergarten just a few weeks when the teacher told the children about picture day and sent a notice home to the parents. Sanguine Rose loved to dress up and have her picture taken. She had pretty dresses and matching ribbons for Easter and Christmas and she could wear one of those for picture day. But the morning of picture day there was no clean dress for her to change into, and Phlegmatic Mom was still asleep. Her mother woke and told her she'd help her get dressed, but she stayed in bed until the bus came. Rose knew from experience not to upset her mother, or her father would punish her later. So she put on her favorite plaid jumper and found ribbons to match in the bathroom. She put some extra effort into putting her own hair into pigtails and went off to school, feeling pretty and a little proud that she had made herself so beautiful for picture day.

When Rose got to school, though, she noticed that all her playmates had perfect pinafores and curly hairdos that looked like they came out of a fashion magazine. They were gorgeous, and it was obvious that they had received extra attention and special treatment from their mothers. Suddenly Rose didn't feel so beautiful. She ran to the bathroom to try to fix the crooked part in her hair, and a mother who was fussing over her own daughter took pity on Rose. She put some barrettes in her hair to keep the strays from falling in her face, but it was too late.

Rose's kindergarten picture will always show a forced smile and a pitiful little face that says, "Please *don't* look at me."

Phlegmatic parents need to learn to put effort into helping their Sanguine children be the adorable princes and princesses they long to be. Picture time is especially important to Sanguines. Fix them up special and send them off with an encouraging word and an air of confidence.

Whatever your personality type, if you have a Sanguine child, learn to appreciate your child's good humor and lively temperament. Help him or her learn to fill in the weaknesses in his or her personality by emphasizing the importance of balancing responsibility and organization with fun and excitement. Let your Sanguines have fun but teach them they need goals and discipline to succeed. And above all, expect your child to surprise you. Every day will be an exciting adventure!

five

CHARACTERISTICS OF A CONTROLLING CHOLERIC

CHOLERIC

Powerful Personality

The Extrovert • The Leader • The Optimist

Emotional needs: appreciation for all achievements, opportunity for leadership, participation in family decisions, something to control (own room, garage, backyard, dog)

Avoids: rest, boredom, playing games she can't win

Strengths	Weaknesses
BABY	
• bright and wide-eyed	• strong-willed
• adventuresome	• demanding
• energetic	• loud
• outgoing	• throws things
• precocious	• not sleepy
• born leader	

Strengths	Weaknesses
CHILD	
• daring and eager	• manipulative
• productive worker	• temper tantrums
• sees the goal	• constantly going
• moves quickly	• insistent
• self-sufficient	• testing
• competitive	• arguing
• assertive	• stubborn
• trustworthy	
TEEN	
• aggressive	• too bossy
• competent	• controls parents
• organizes well	• knows everything
• assumes leadership	• looks down on "dummies"
• problem solver	• unpopular
• self-confident	• may become a leader
• stimulates others	• insulting
• excels in emergencies	• judgmental
• great potential	• unrepentant
• responsible	

While babysitting her three-year-old grandson at his home, Marilyn suggested they straighten up his disastrous room as a surprise for his mommy. He said, "Dat's a dood idea!" (Translated, that means, "That's a good idea!") In the process, she handed him a toy and asked him to put it in his toy box. He said, "No, I tan't do dat." When his grandmother asked why, he said proudly, "I'm the in-charge guy."

Already at three, he understood the supervisory position!

If there were one personality that could prove we are, in fact, born with a direction of behavior, it would be the Choleric child.

Right from the beginning this little one knows she will take control of the whole family; it is just a matter of when. I remember one visit to a friend with a new baby. The child was next to her in a bassinet, and every so often she let out a scream. She wasn't crying for a bottle, though; she was screaming for control. And she got it. Her mother would always immediately look over and say, "What shall I do?" The baby knew from the beginning that she could be in charge! These take-charge children do, however, have some important emotional needs that are very different from all the others.

Appreciation and Control

As we have seen, the Sanguine is looking for attention and approval from everyone. The Choleric doesn't care what anybody thinks as long as she gets credit and *appreciation* for everything she does for those who don't seem to be doing anything at all.

Choleric children will be your greatest helpers if you thank them and praise them for their accomplishments. They think in terms of work and must be busy to feel good about themselves. If you don't give them something to do, they'll fix something you didn't even know was broken. Gainfully occupied, they will stay out of trouble; but idle, they may become the chief of mischief makers. They like to hear comments such as, "I can't believe how quickly you cleaned up your room" or "You get more done than anyone I know."

In addition to praise for good works Cholerics need to feel you are on their side and loyal to their cause. They see life in black and white, with an it's-my-way-or-the-highway attitude. You are either with these children or against them. If you're with them, you'll get along just fine. But if you're against them, watch out! It's best to be loyal to their side.

Cholerics also want to know you understand their need for *control.* If they are put down at home and not considered a productive part of the family, they may go out and beat up their peers or take over from the teacher in school. The Choleric child loves to get a reaction out of you, and getting you really angry is worth the spanking.

Sue was a loving, easygoing mother with a Choleric child named Terry. By the time Terry was three years old, Sue was already worn out by his refusal to obey, his high energy level, and his joy in driving her to the brink. As she lay on the couch watching him play, he went to the record cabinet and pulled out the old LPs she'd never bothered to get rid of. He seemed happy emptying them all out of their jackets, so she didn't object until he spread them all over the carpet and began to dance on top of them.

Sue commanded him to stop, but that only energized him more. Finally, Sue got off the couch and yelled at him. Terry was thrilled he'd gotten her to stand up and he danced more dramatically, waving his little hands in the air. Sue was beside herself, but her yelling had absolutely no effect.

Sue had to learn to take charge of Terry at the first sign of trouble and not lock herself away. The Choleric child needs to be *appreciated* and needs something to *control*—his toys, his room, the wastebaskets, the dog, the laundry—but make sure it isn't you!

Let's Make the Rules

Cholerics know there is a need for rules in life but they want to be the ones to make them. In fact, they firmly believe that rules are theirs to make and that the rest of us should be grateful for their direction. From the time he was two, Dallas knew his grandmother didn't "do things right." When they got in the car, Dallas would say, "Put your seatbelt on, Grammy! Do you have enough gas? Is it on F or E? Aren't you going too fast? It should be on 3 and 0. Put both your hands on the wheel. Don't turn around to talk when you're driving! You could crack me up!" Young Dallas had no idea that it was his grandmother who was being cracked up.

One day when Dallas was three, he and his dad picked up his grandparents at the airport. As they got into the car, the child pointed and told his grandfather, "You get in the front seat with my daddy and you two talk together. Grammy and I will have a private time in the back." Everyone sat where Dallas said and followed his rules until Grandpa, forgetting the instructions momentarily, asked Grandma a question. Instantly Dallas spoke up, "Save that until you get home, Pop! Remember the rules!"

Encourage the Choleric to see structure in life and make rules and goals for her own activities, but don't let her make your schedule just because she is precocious.

My Way's the Only Way

To say that Choleric children have a mind of their own would be putting it mildly. They are determined to do things on their terms. When Lauren was five years old, she took dancing lessons. For the recital, a group was doing a mini-Rockettes number and Lauren was the last one to tap off the stage. At the recital, the girl in front of Lauren didn't move fast enough, and without missing a beat, Lauren smiled at the audience and shoved the girl right off into the wings. That will teach anyone to get in her way!

Another mother told me about three-year-old Courtney's dance recital. In the middle of the group number, Courtney got sick of dancing and sat down right in the center of the stage. The teacher tried to call her off, but she wouldn't move until the dance was over. Then she stood up, bowed, and danced off with the others.

No matter the event, Cholerics are determined to do things their way. They'll not play follow-the-leader unless they're setting the pace. It's their way or no way!

Choleric Johnny had been misbehaving and was sent to his room. After a while he emerged and informed his mother that he had thought it over and then said a prayer. "Fine," responded his pleased mother. "If you ask God to help you not misbehave, he will help you." Without missing a beat, Johnny replied, "Oh, I didn't ask him to help me not misbehave. I asked him to help you put up with me." Cholerics are determined to make the rest of the world dance to the beat of *their* drum!

Perfect . . . When They Want to Be

Choleric children aren't perfectionists like the Melancholies but they want things right when they're important to them. What's "right" can be different with each child, and the areas in which this child decides to be picky are obvious at an early age.

Little Susie's first word was "no," and she used it loudly to get her own way. When sitting in her high chair she would not eat until all the cabinet doors in the kitchen were closed. It took a while for her mother to understand that Susie's screaming and pointing to the wall meant, "I will not eat until you shut the doors." Once Susie was big enough to reach the shelf in her bedroom she placed all her stuffed toys in order. If her mother moved them around while cleaning and Susie found them out of line, she would yell and point until her mother came in and rearranged them to suit her. Susie had more than her toys in line!

If I Can't Win, I Won't Play!

Cholerics want activity that is challenging and exciting and most of all where they can win. Their motto is, "If I can't win, I won't play!" They like to be the best at whatever they touch and love to set records. They will be team players if they see they will be able to stand out, but blending in doesn't appeal to them. They like power sports where they can show their strength. Because of their inborn desire to control, they usually rise quickly to the top of whatever they join. Bev remembers the first time she and her husband took their kids bowling. They were only in the second frame of the very first game, and already Anna was depressed because she wasn't doing very well. She came over to the table and exclaimed, "I'm going to lose! This is terrible!" Bev tried to encourage her, saying, "We just started; I thought we were here to have fun!" But her daughter shook her head and responded, "I'm not here to have fun; I'm here to win! I thought bowling was something I could win!"

Take It to the Limit

Cholerics love to test you and see what they can get away with. Their minds are always busy and if they see you relax your guard for a second, they will move in for the kill. Mutiny is always a possibility!

When Lauren was in preschool her teacher said to me, "I never have to worry if I can't come to school. Lauren could run the whole place by herself!" My daughter had obviously made many take-over attempts!

Pressing Buttons

Cholerics take fiendish delight in controlling situations that will exasperate their parents. If they can control an activity or put their parents in an embarrassing position, Choleric children think they have made their day. Their mutinous little minds grab onto such possibilities as triumphant experiences.

Kay drove up to the gas station with eighteen-month-old Caroline in the car. Kay got out, leaving the key in the ignition. She filled the tank and went to get in the car only to find that Caroline had pushed the button and locked the doors. Kay started talking sweetly, saying, "Press the button, sweetie, so Mommy can get in the car." Caroline grinned and didn't move. Kay's sweet talk picked up in volume as Caroline refused to let her mom into the car. Soon Kay was screaming bribes such as "I'll buy you ice cream." When Caroline just smiled back, Kay began to bang on the windows, demanding, "Let me in! Let me in!" Soon others came to see why Kay was so hysterical.

One man told Kay, "Calm down. I'll tell her what to do." He started talking softly to Caroline: "Push the little button, honey; just push the button." Caroline would reach toward the button but she wouldn't push it. Soon this man was frustrated also. All around the car, people were yelling to Caroline, who refused to budge. She had never had this much fun before. Finally, one man got a coat hanger and worked the window down enough to press the button. Caroline smiled and said, "Hi!" to her new friend as a humiliated Kay dropped into her seat and drove away. A Choleric child is never too young to delight in getting a whole group of adults under control. Just another pleasant day in paradise!

No Consequences for Me!

Choleric children frequently try to outmanipulate and con their parents, always trying to avoid consequences at all costs. On Mother's Day last year, Diane's nine-year-old daughter Shanna was her usual disobedient, strong-willed self at church. While the family was at a restaurant for lunch after church, Shanna repeatedly asked if she could go to the front where they had gumball and trinket machines. Diane and her husband told her she could not. While they were talking Shanna disappeared to the bathroom—or so her parents thought until she returned with a small bright-colored ball. The ball was quickly confiscated and an edict was issued that Shanna would spend an hour in her room when the family got home. Shanna responded that she didn't mind because she was sleepy and wanted to take a nap. Cholerics never let the threat of punishment appear to bother them because they are already plotting revenge.

At home later Diane enjoyed a peaceful afternoon without a peep out of either of her kids. Only when she heard Shanna's cries did she realize things hadn't been as peaceful as they'd seemed. Rather than spend the afternoon in her room, as she'd been instructed, Shanna had gone outside and locked herself in the trunk of the car, confident that her mother would come looking for her. Unfortunately for Shanna, her plan backfired and instead of scaring her mother, she scared herself when no one came after her. Cholerics will go to nearly any extreme to do things on their terms!

Act Now, Think Later

Choleric children don't need to think things over. They move quickly into action. My mother didn't usually give me advice about raising my children, but she did tell them what she thought I should be doing. Marita had long, fine hair, and I kept it in a ponytail with a rubber band holding it in place at the crown of her head. While combing Marita's hair, my mother would frequently suggest, "Why doesn't your mother cut your hair?" Four-year-old Marita soon tired of Grammy's suggestions; one day she walked into the kitchen with scissors in one hand and her ponytail in the other. I screamed at the sight as she handed me the swag of hair with the rubber band still on it and said, "Here, Grammy said my hair was too long. So I cut it!"

Three-year-old Kay cut off one pigtail, then approached her mother with the tail in one hand and a bottle of glue in the other. When her mother almost fainted, Kay assured her, "Don't worry, I glue it on!"

Choleric children don't worry about anything. They figure there's always a solution!

Where Are Your Manners?

Teaching children manners has always been an important issue for parents. With Choleric children, it can take some extra effort to see that you've succeeded. At the dinner table one night, two-year-old Heather yelled out, "More milk, more milk!" in a demanding voice. Dad gave his daughter a stern look, filled the cup with milk, and holding firmly onto the glass, pushed it toward her, asking, "What do you say when you ask for something?" Expecting to hear a contrite "please," he was taken aback when his two-year-old put her hand on the glass, looked him square in the eyes, and said, *"Let go!"*

Bijan gave his grandmother an equally difficult time. One day he came dashing into the kitchen ordering, "Coke! Coke! Coke!" She responded, "You may have a Coke, but what do you say first?" Quickly Bijan responded, "Peese." (He had trouble with *l*s.) His grandmother poured the soft drink and handed him the glass, then asked, "Now what do you say?" He smiled, obviously knowing the right answer, held his glass aloft, and called out, "Cheers!"

Even when Cholerics know what they are to do, they often won't give you the satisfaction of responding correctly. It's just so much fun to catch you off guard.

Practice What You Preach

Choleric children don't always follow their own advice. My Choleric grandson Bryan, at age thirteen, frequently stormed to his room and slammed the door when things didn't go his way. He'd hide away and not talk to anyone. Imagine my daughter's surprise when she heard him counseling a friend on the phone. "You know what your problem is? You spend no quality time interacting with your family." Help your child see the inconsistencies in her behavior and words by making sure you practice what you preach.

Confident or Cocky?

Cholerics dream big dreams and are confident they can achieve them. Tennis star Martina Hingis is a typical Choleric. Confident, sometimes cocky, she talks proudly of herself, and many believe her to be arrogant. Chris Evert has said she's never seen panic or fear in the younger woman's eyes. Martina's mother, Melanie Molitor, named her after Martina Navratilova and "steered her down the path to wealth and stardom." As she says, "The dream of every parent is to get your child to be the best that they can be in whatever they do."[4] But would Martina's mother have been as successful in raising a superstar daughter if Martina had not been born with the Choleric drive to win?

When not curbed in any way, Cholerics can become so confident that they overwhelm friends and even adults. When they are toddlers, their confidence is considered precocious; but as they grow up, it can become arrogance. As parents, we need to teach them the difference between being confident or cute and being cocky.

six

PARENTING YOUR CHOLERIC CHILD

Parents of a Choleric child must brace themselves for a power struggle from day one. These children are born ready to take charge. Properly channel their natural leadership skills and you'll help propel them to success.

Since these born leaders know they are in charge from the moment of birth,they will look for things to control. If you don't give this child charge of something that it's appropriate for him to control, he'll take charge of whatever comes his way—including you!

From early childhood Cholerics know they are right. At age three my grandson Bryan was playing a game with Fred and was not playing by the rules. When Fred pointed out Bryan's error, the boy instantly countered, "I am not wrong. I am right." While it's true that Cholerics are the individuals most apt to make correct judgments, you'll need to teach your Choleric children to make sure they aren't "playing by their own rules."

Like Sanguines, Powerful Cholerics tend to blurt things out without concern for someone else's feelings. They don't deliberately mean to hurt others, but they aren't very sensitive to the feelings of those around them. In fact, their practical nature tends to make them look the other way rather than showing compassion toward or spending time with those who might be hurting. Help your child improve his sensitivity to others and develop a heart for the hurting.

Every parent with a Choleric child will discover that strong parental leadership is critical for your family's health. You'll want to develop your children's leadership abilities and allow them a measure of control, but make sure they realize you're the one in charge of the family. How you accomplish that task depends on your personality as a parent.

Popular Parent with a Powerful Child

Popular Parents will enjoy the strengths of their high-achieving Powerful children. They'll brag about their kids' achievements and willingly share the spotlight in any honors. The double optimistic outlook of this combination and the parent's willingness to give the child the praise he so desires make this a strong team. The problem comes when this driven child senses the parent's lack of resolve and takes control of the adult's life.

Who's in Charge Here?

Popular parents may allow a shift of control to their children because these parents don't like to work and because they so desperately need to be loved that they'll do anything to avoid problem situations where they might be unpopular. Being a parent means you won't always be liked by your headstrong Choleric children, but if you don't establish firm boundaries, you may find your roles being reversed.

Sometimes Sanguine parents actually allow their Choleric children to dictate the time they wish to be picked up and accept their reprimands for being late. When she was six, my Choleric daughter Lauren got tired of my forgetting her kindergarten share time. She picked out three weeks' worth of share time items and put them safely in the car. She decided that if I wouldn't make sure things got done, she'd do it for me!

An Inch Given, a Mile Taken

When a Sanguine mother has a teenage Choleric son, the son often becomes protective of his poor, mixed-up mother. But a Choleric daughter may look at her Sanguine mother in despair, take over control of the house, and become her father's best friend.

When Choleric children observe a Sanguine father's vulnerability, they quickly learn to cleverly flatter him into getting their own way, their own car, and extra money. The Popular parent must always be aware that the Powerful child is out to capture new territories, slay a few dragons, and take over the throne.

Let Me "Help" You

It's natural for Choleric children to conclude that they are smarter than their Sanguine parents. Sanguine Kathy's motto is: Look good; fake smart. Her son Graham easily sees through the "fake smart" part and constantly helps her get her act together. One day Kathy was hunting for her sunglasses and was tearing around in a panic. "What are you missing this time?" Graham asked in a condescending tone.

When informed it was a pair of sunglasses that was creating the commotion, Graham took Kathy by the hand and led her to the kitchen. He pointed to her glasses on top of the flour canister.

He matter-of-factly stated, "You always put them there. You come in wearing them, go straight to the kitchen to unload your groceries, realize it's dark in there, take off your glasses, and put them on the flour canister. Anyone knows they don't go there and it doesn't make any sense, but that's what you do. Is there anything else you're missing?"

If they're not careful, Sanguine parents will find their Choleric children lacking respect for them. And their dependence on their capable children will lead to a role reversal that further deteriorates the child's confidence in the parent.

Powerful Parent with a **Powerful Child**

This powerful combination's strengths lie in their drive for success, ability to achieve, and willingness to be responsible for the rest of the family. Together, these self-motivated, outgoing people can accomplish just about anything. It may be a bumpy ride, though, given their feisty, volatile nature and their absolute need to win every battle. If these two don't see eye to eye or compromise their positions, life becomes a battleground and other family members become casualties.

Closeness or Exclusiveness?

Ideally, Choleric parent and child will agree on a goal and march toward it together. For example, a strong, athletic father may produce a son with similar desires, and they can mutually dedicate their lives to sports. Such closeness is desirable for the parent and child, but the pair must be careful that their mutual goals and admiration don't lead to exclusiveness that shuts out other family members.

John Sr. had a Powerful personality. He set his standards for what a real man did and tolerated nothing less. Either you fit his mold or you were wrong. Since he owned his own business, no one bucked him for control. His family had been dominating forces in his church for generations and were the largest single financial supporters, so he spoke with an unquestioned voice of authority in church.

When his oldest son and namesake didn't share his "masculine" interests, John Sr. cast his older son aside and concentrated on his second son, Rick. While John Jr. hated anything to do with shooting and was allergic to just about everything growing in the woods, Rick loved going out in the woods with his father, and guns fascinated him. This sport helped bind these two together, but it eliminated John Sr.'s relationship with his firstborn.

John Jr. shared with me that his father had let him know from the beginning that he would never be a "real man" if he didn't love the outdoors. Every time the two hunters would head for the woods, John was told, "It's too bad you aren't coming with us." The demeaning tone of his father's statement made John feel like a wimp. His mother babied and consoled him, keeping him in the house with her.

John's musical talent found him cast in singing roles in school productions, something his father scoffed at, believing that being in plays could have no positive impact for a boy. "That's sissy stuff," he remarked. "Once I'd seen him in leotards dancing like an elf, I refused to go again. I couldn't stomach my son in that fruity stuff. His mother has made a fool out of him!"

Here was a strong, intellectual, successful businessman and church elder who had been able to control everything he touched in life but this one son. A typical Choleric, he was without any insight as to how he might have contributed to his son's "utter failure to grow up to be a man."

Powerful parents must learn to take off single-minded blinders and realize that just because someone is different, it doesn't make the person wrong. It's so natural for this strong personality to look at her personal successes and harshly judge those square pegs who don't fit into the Choleric's round holes. When the misfit is her own child, this attitude can have disastrous results.

Constant Clashing

While some Choleric parents and children find themselves working perfectly in tandem with each other, sometimes the opposite happens. Both are determined to win and they may be at each other's throat. Neither will give in because each is certain he or she is right. These two battling Powerful personalities must be brought to the bargaining table. Such a meeting will often look something like peace talks with warring nations, so you'll need to set down some rules of conciliation. You may even need an outside authority, perhaps an intervention or confrontation therapist, to point out the damage such clashing does to the individuals and the family unit. Seldom do these two individuals come to a meeting of the minds on their own initiative!

Despite your personal tendency to fight back, as a parent, you cannot allow constant scrapping for control to become the norm. Instead, discuss areas of dissension, set down working rules, and stick to them. Remember that when you as the parent argue, the children have already won because they got you to enter the fray. You'll need to teach your children the art of compromise by modeling it yourself.

I Give Up!

If the Choleric parent and child are neither walking closely in one accord nor constantly clawing at each other's throats, it's likely that one of them has given up, put on a mask, and pretended not to care. This may appear to be a peaceful solution for the one who wins control, but such peace can't last. Some unexpected day the lid will blow and everyone around will be hit by the flying pieces. I know one Powerful parent who was in control of everything but her young daughter. The child was powerfully precocious and managed to overwhelm even a strong mother. The child made decisions for herself, told her brothers and sisters what to wear each day, and chose the restaurants where the family ate.

One day when she reprimanded her mother for having failed to feed the dog on time, something snapped. The mother suddenly realized she had allowed this child to change positions with her. She became so furious that she slapped the child, banging her head against the wall in the process. The child couldn't imagine why her mother went so wild when she had only mentioned the dog was hungry.

Whenever we completely sublimate our natural personality for any period of time, it will come bursting out when we least expect it. To avoid the outburst, you must come to a mutual understanding of why both Choleric family members desire control and you must discuss the division of authority in the family. It'll spare your whole family a lot of grief if you do!

Perfect Parent with a **Powerful Child**

The Melancholy parent and Choleric child share a natural ability to organize and keep on schedule. The child wants to do what's right in his own sight, and if that coordinates with the parent's perfectionist nature the relationship will do well. Unlike the Sanguine child, the Choleric knows what day of the week it is and can usually outthink his parents. The parent's aim should not be to shut down this child's leadership ability but to keep the two of you on the same side. Keeping this in mind, emphasize points on which you agree and constantly remind the child how much you appreciate his help in running the family. With steady affirmation of the work he is doing, the Choleric will remain committed to high achievement and will do half of your work for you. This child will even remember to check off his chart and do odd jobs you didn't assign! Remember, though, that this child needs recognition for such effort.

Giving Credit Where Credit Is Due

If you don't understand your child's need for credit, you'll find yourself in trouble. If you and your child end up on opposing teams, you'll enter a battle you may never win. The Choleric child can become instantly devious and manipulative and can inspire dedicated loyalty from those he selects to oppose you.

Despite this hazard, don't throw up your hands in despair. To be forewarned is to be forearmed in this case. Your superachieving child needs to have daily challenges and constant affirmation. Such treatment doesn't come naturally for the Melancholy who typically reserves praise only for jobs perfectly completed and often tinges compliments with criticism ("that's great, *but* . . ."). If you recognize this difference between you and your child, however, you can learn to separate your praise and instruction, and ask yourself, *Is insisting on perfection worth the risk?*

You may fear, as my mother did, that giving compliments will give your child a "swelled head." But since your young Cholerics will only stay on your side if they know you appreciate what they've done for you, the absence of compliments may cause mutiny. Seeing your child from this perspective will help you appreciate the value of meeting your child's emotional needs and keeping him on your team!

God Can't Do It That Fast!

When it comes to discipline, Choleric children are immensely stubborn. Don't expect that just because you've developed a reasonable Melancholy response to your child's misbehavior that the results will always be what you expect—or that they'll come *when* you expect them.

Debby's Melancholy mom was a meticulous housekeeper. When Debby was a young child, they lived in an apartment on the second story of a very old house. The floors were not carpeted, but her mom had rugs scattered throughout the house. Debby was a typical Choleric tyke—always into things, always messing things up, always active.

One day Debby's mom had had it. After admonishing her daughter many times to be quiet and be a "good girl," she finally gave up. The last straw came when she stepped back to admire her perfectly dusted floor and found her darling, grinning monster on her knees right behind her messing up the rugs and dropping cookie crumbs along her trail.

"Debby Ogle—you are going to take a nap right now!" she pronounced as she swooped up her daughter and put her into bed. "Now you kneel down and ask God to make you a good little girl!"

Debby knelt down and timidly asked God to make her a good little girl, but the instant her mother closed the door to her room, Debby began hollering. Her mother flung open the door to find all of Debby's stuffed animals tossed helter-skelter all over the room, along with her blanket and pillow. This "good little girl" was bouncing up and down on her bed screaming with delight!

"Debby, What are you doing? You just asked God to make you a good little girl!" her mother demanded. Delightedly bouncing, Debby shrieked back, "He can't do it that fast!"

Be aware that your strong-willed, controlling Cholerics will want to establish their own timetable for obedience!

Peaceful Parent with a **Powerful Child**

Perhaps the most exhausting combination is the Peaceful parent who wants to stay calm, cool, and collected with one or more Powerful children who want constant control and instant action.

This parent-child combination can complement each other if the naturally reticent parent establishes control from the beginning and relinquishes areas of control only when the child has matured enough to appropriately handle them. The greatest hazard for this combination comes when the parent's weakness in the area of discipline allows the child to have all the power in a situation even before he or she really understands the meaning of the word!

Sharon's first child had been Peaceful right from the beginning, totally undemanding, and loving to sleep. Her second baby was exactly the opposite—controlling right from the start. He would nurse only from one side; the minute Sharon put him on the other breast, he would push away and scream. Each feeding she would start him on the "wrong side" and he would yell and push. Then she'd shift him to the other side. Sharon recalls how she would wait an extra hour until he was so hungry he was eating his fists and he still refused to nurse from the "wrong side." This Powerful baby was determined from birth that he would control his mother and he did. For a whole year his mother looked like a lopsided camel!

Out of Balance

Often with the Phlegmatic-Choleric combination, the balance is tilted in the wrong direction. The child has an inner mechanism that is certain control can be obtained by persistent determination.

When Peaceful Brenda gave birth to Michael, everyone assumed he'd be calm and Phlegmatic like his parents. But right from the beginning he surprised them all. Before he could talk, he grunted and pointed directions with his finger. His first full sentence was "I can do it myself." By the time Michael was two, he was in charge and his parents were checking their decisions with him. One day Brenda was on the floor playing with him and she asked, "May I get up, Michael?" He replied instantly, "Just sit down and be a nice lady." Brenda sat down. Michael's younger sister has followed in his footsteps. Not quite two, Heidi pulls her mother into the right spot and points to a seat. If Brenda sits somewhere else, Heidi tugs on her again until she gets her own way.

Brenda said she has to force herself each morning to make strong statements and establish authority, setting the tone for the day. If she weakens anywhere along the line, Michael and Heidi are both poised for the kill. They don't even have to think about it; they instinctively take control.

Oh Well, It Won't Kill Him

Choleric children love Phlegmatic parents because they are easygoing and pleasant to get along with and they don't really care what the child is doing. I remember my mother saying, "I don't care what you do as long as I can't see it or hear it."

At an Easter Sunday family gathering, I noticed my two-year-old grandson Bryan sitting on the grass next to Marita's two Schnauzer puppies and their dish of food. As Bryan began to feed them, I saw that he was putting one piece of kibble into each puppy's mouth and then one into his own little mouth. I pointed this out to my son-in-law Randy.

"Don't do that, Bryan. Don't eat the dog's food, little Bryan," Randy said softly. Bryan looked him straight in the eye, picked up one more piece, stuck it in his mouth, and smiled at his father. Randy merely shrugged and said to me, "Oh well, a little dog food won't kill him."

It's always easier for the Peaceful parent not to buck the Powerful child, but a smart, aggressive child will control more than you bargained for if you allow it.

Slow Boil, Big Explosion

Phlegmatic parents have to be careful that by avoiding effort or conflict, they don't suppress what truly bothers them until they blow. Serena sat at her computer while her three toddlers ran around the kitchen. Out of the corner of her eye she could see her Choleric daughter Kristin crawling up the counters to reach the cookie jar. Serena wanted her daughter to get down but first tried to ignore her behavior because she didn't want to stop what she was doing to get up for what she knew would be a battle. Calmly Serena called out, "Kristin, get down." Kristin ignored her and kept climbing. Serena repeated her warning with a little more authority in her voice and a threat, "Kristin, come down now or you will get a spanking." Kristin ignored her again. Serena was irritated but was too tired to take on her daughter in an argument. Still hoping she wouldn't have to get up, Serena tried another warning in a louder voice and added, "I really mean it!" When Kristin continued, Serena's heart began to race and she felt her face flush as the anger rose up inside her. Finally, as Kristin reached the cookie jar, Serena jumped out of her chair, almost knocked the computer off the desk, and grabbed Kristin, smacking her across the face and screaming, "Get down right now!" Now all the kids were crying. Serena had lost control and was both angry and ashamed at her abusive behavior to her daughter.

In an effort to avoid arguments or conflict, Phlegmatic parents have to be careful that they don't allow their anger to build. Part of the solution is learning how to overcome the natural tendency to ignore the situation and to avoid any effort in solving the problem. Serena learned that she needed to give her children one warning and then make the effort to stop what she was doing, get up out of her chair, and take action before her anger built.

Easier Isn't Healthier

It's easier for a Phlegmatic parent to forgo healthy boundaries for their strong-willed children, but it does a lot of emotional damage in the long run. Phlegmatic Stephanie, divorced mother of three-year-old Choleric Victoria, lives with her father. From the time she could crawl, Victoria has been in charge of the household because neither her mom nor her grandfather like to set or enforce boundaries. It's easier to give Victoria her way. Unfortunately, when they visit friends and Victoria starts her selfish, demanding behavior, others don't want any of them around. Although Victoria is a bright, adorable, curly-haired beauty, no one likes her because no one is parenting her properly.

Phlegmatic parents need to be careful that they don't focus only on providing the easy things, like dinner, laundry, or transportation to school and back. Lack of setting and enforcing healthy boundaries may become emotional deprivation and set a child up for a lifetime of rejection.

I Knew I Could Get to You!

Choleric kids are notorious for knowing how to push anyone's buttons, but they're especially adept at doing so with the normally easygoing Phlegmatic. Ashley was preparing to leave and told her daughter Lauren to get her wagon out from behind the car so that they could go. She was in a hurry and wanted Lauren to get it done immediately. When Ashley returned from a last dash into the house, there was Lauren, sitting in a child's lawn chair behind the car, sunglasses on, arms folded across her chest, her long legs crossed. Just sitting there, she was! Ashley raised her voice a few decibels and said, "Lauren! Didn't I tell you that I wanted you to be ready to go in the car when I came out again?!" Lauren slowly and carefully took her sunglasses off and said to her mom, "I knew this would aggravate you and sure enough it did."

Self-Parented Children

Choleric children often take on the role of parent to their mother or father, consequently parenting themselves through life. This form of rejection can leave the child feeling emotionally abandoned.

Golden's Phlegmatic mom played the role of child to her Choleric daughter. In her drunken father's absence, Golden naturally assumed the parental role. From the time she was young, Golden made all her own decisions. The family had no car, so she had to find rides any time she wanted to go anywhere. She set her own curfews, piano practice times, and homework schedule, and she searched out scholarships and got herself to college. Later she planned and paid for her own wedding. She looked forward to her husband coming alongside her and taking care of her for a change.

Golden's mother is in her twilight years now, and nothing has changed. She still depends on her daughter to make all the decisions. Golden knows her mother did the best she could based on the situation she was in, given her Phlegmatic temperament. But that doesn't erase the emotional pain at having missed out on the support she craved as a child.

Taking Care of Yourself

Phlegmatic parents can become exhausted trying to take charge of their Choleric children. One woman passed the cookie section of the grocery store with her three-year-old daughter. When the child whined for cookies, her mother told her "no." The little girl immediately began to fuss even louder and the mother said quietly, "Now, Ellen, we just have half the aisles left to go through. Don't be upset. It won't be long."

Later, in the candy aisle, the little girl began to shout for candy. When she was told "no," she again began to cry loudly. This time the mother responded, "There, there, Ellen, don't cry. Only two more aisles to go and we'll be checking out."

Finally at the checkout counter, the little girl began to clamor for gum and burst into a terrible tantrum when her mother again said "no." The mother patiently said, "Ellen, we'll be through this line in a few minutes and then you can go home and have a nice nap."

A man who had witnessed each step of the drama followed them out to the parking lot and stopped the woman to compliment her on her patience with little Ellen. The mother broke in, "My little girl's name is Tammy. I'm Ellen."

If you're drained by the efforts of controlling your children, make sure you get enough rest and time for yourself. Sometimes parents' needs come first.

Choleric children will keep any parent on his or her toes. Their drive and passion for leadership will challenge even strong parents. To keep a proper balance in your parent-child relationship, give your Cholerics control over certain areas in their lives but be sure to let them know who has the last word.

seven

MARKS OF A METICULOUS MELANCHOLY

MELANCHOLY

Perfect Personality

The Introvert • The Thinker • The Pessimist

Emotional needs: sensitivity to deep desires, satisfaction from quality achievement, space to call her own, security and stability, separation from noisy or messy siblings, support from parents

Avoids: noise, confusion, trivial pursuits, being jollied

Strengths	Weaknesses
BABY	
• serious	• suspicious/guarded
• quiet	• shy/closed
• likes a schedule	• looks sad
• analyzes others	• cries easily
• content alone	• clings

Strengths	Weaknesses
CHILD	
• thinks deeply	• moody
• talented	• whines
• musical	• self-conscious
• fantasizes	• too sensitive
• true friend	• hears negatives
• perfectionist	• avoids criticism
• intense	• sees problems
• dutiful and responsible	• won't communicate
TEEN	
• thinks deeply	• depressed and withdrawn
• good student	• inferiority complex
• creative—likes research	• inflexible
• organized and purposeful	• suspicious of people
• high standards	• critical
• conscientious and on time	• negative attitude
• neat and orderly	• poor self-image
• sensitive to others	• revengeful
• sweet spirit	• lives through friends
• thrifty	• needs approval

From the time David sat up in his high chair, he has been a picky eater. He would frequently scream when he looked at the food his mother was placing before him. At first she didn't know what he was trying to communicate, but when one of his first words was "no" and the second was "touch," she began to see what he was pointing at. He couldn't stand having his potatoes touch his peas!

Exactly the opposite of the Sanguine personality is the Melancholy individual. Even as a baby the Perfect Melancholy appears to be thinking deeply. Melancholies are quiet and undemanding and they like to be alone. They follow schedules from the beginning and respond well to an organized environment. My son Fred has been an extraordinary Melancholy since birth—always analyzing, constantly serious, unquestionably reliable, and ever introspective. As young Fred grew up, it became more obvious to me just how different his personality was from my own.

Four S's

Where Sanguines look for attention from the outside, Melancholies desire sensitivity about what's inside. They don't talk about their needs; instead, they are quite determined that if you really love them, you will figure out their problems. The more they are pushed to talk, the more they clam up until you are ready to scream. This attitude shows them you are not sensitive and are not on their side. When they are depressed, they want your dedicated *sensitivity* and *support,* but your impulse may be just to tell them to cheer up and get on with life.

Melancholies also need *space* of their own where they can keep their things in order. They go into a decline when a little brother or sister touches their things. They are not being difficult, they just need a place to call their own. My daughter Lauren met her son Randy's Melancholy needs by giving him a room by himself and allowing him to have a hook-lock high on the outside of the door to keep his inquisitive brothers out. If at all possible, allow your Melancholy children to have separate rooms, being sensitive to their emotional needs and not making fun of them. If these children perceive that you think they are a little odd, they'll tune you out and eliminate communication.

As well as *space* a Melancholy must have a place of *silence* where she can go to get over the impact of the noisy people she has encountered during the day. While a Sanguine child will come home and entertain you with stories of the day, the Melancholy doesn't want to even think about it. The Melancholy's response is, "Leave me alone. Let me go to my room and think."

For Melancholies, then, *sensitivity, support, space,* and *silence* are the necessities of their lives.

Where's the Beef?

Melancholies like everything to be in order but they're not always willing to tell others what they want to see done. They assume that others will notice their pain and be sensitive enough to straighten out whatever problem exists, preferring to suffer in silence rather than tell anyone what bothers them.

After more than twenty-eight years of marriage, Bunny learned that her husband likes his meat directly in front of him on the dinner plate. Not on the side of the plate, or the back of the plate, but on the front of the plate. For years he faithfully but quietly turned his plate around so that the meat entrée was in front of him before starting to eat his dinner. Rather than complain, he simply dealt with the inconvenience, and it took his wife nearly thirty years to notice!

Say *Exactly* What You Mean

The Melancholy child is apt to take everything you say at face value. When Melancholy Wesley was four years old, he was watching TV with his father. During a commercial his dad commented, "Are you ever a lucky boy to have color television! When I was a boy, we only had black and white."

After a few minutes of contemplating his dad's statement, Wesley looked at him with total confusion and worry, then asked, "Even in crayons?"

Don't ridicule your children for asking what seem to be unnecessary questions. Instead, remember their need to truly understand and they will be more likely to appreciate all you have to say.

What Are You Asking?

Precise Melancholies will answer exactly the question you ask, not necessarily tell you what you want to find out. When Melancholy Alan was eight years old, he was invited to spend the night at a friend's house. The next morning his friend's mother said to Alan, "I'm going to run down to the store. What kind of sweet rolls does your mother give you for breakfast?" Alan quickly replied, "Oh, my mother buys the kind with raisins on it." Satisfied with his response, the mother purchased frosted sweet rolls with raisins and served them to the children when she returned home. As she turned to get the milk from the refrigerator, she saw Alan methodically removing the raisins from his sweet roll and sticking them on the edge of his plate. Puzzled, she asked, "Alan, didn't you say those were the sweet rolls your mother always buys?" He simply replied, "Oh, they are. I just don't like the raisins."

When you want to get information out of your Melancholy child, ask pointed questions. Don't assume this child will tell you what you want to know unless you know how to ask her to specifically do so.

Neatniks

Melancholies are both neat and creative. In fact, they are always creating new ways to be neat. Lane remembers how her Aunt Jackie kept the neatest house of anyone in their family. Everything had its proper place and the meticulous care of everything and everyone was mind-boggling. She was always devising time- or energy-saving solutions to things the rest of the family didn't even see as problems.

Aunt Jackie's neatness caused tension, though, on family vacations. She couldn't stand luggage. It was messy—it was in the way and bulky and unsightly in the home of other relatives. She didn't want to be a problem but she couldn't keep those suitcases neat and in order! Her three children would rake through the perfectly folded clothes in their suitcases, and all her work would be ruined, wrinkled, or tossed out on the floor.

Aunt Jackie couldn't stand this lack of concern for order very long. To solve this, she devised a solution. Instead of taking the messy suitcases inside, she would leave them in the car and carefully retrieve what was needed when it was called for. Her children were not allowed out to the car themselves, and they needed a good excuse to get her to retrieve their clothes. Eventually Aunt Jackie was able to eliminate suitcases completely, instead providing a small, neatly cut, open-top cardboard box for each child. Each box was measured so that they all fit together perfectly in the trunk of the car. They didn't jiggle around or have spaces in which to lose things. Each box contained everything the child needed on the trip. No more mess in the house, no more suitcases to open and close in the car, no more children creating havoc, no more children even having access to their own possessions. This neat, creative solution would make Heloise smile, I'm sure. But it nearly drove Aunt Jackie's Sanguine family crazy!

Orderliness

Most Melancholy children are easily bothered by clutter and chaos and are compelled to correct the situation. Some may become genuinely distressed and unable to function unless they are able and allowed to get things back in order.

Suzy's eight-year-old son Keegan brought 110 of his crayons home from school. When his mother asked him why he was keeping only ten colors at school, he replied, "They were making my desk too cluttered. I like to have it more organized so I can see some open space."

Another time Keegan was walking down the church hall on his way to vacation Bible school class. He reached into the boys' room and turned out the bathroom light. When his mom shot him a questioning glance he informed her: "Someone left it on, Mom."

Wherever these children go, they'll find things that need to be put back in order and they'll take the initiative to correct them.

When Will That Happen?

Melancholy children have a profound need to know when things are supposed to happen. They're lost without a schedule and can't be consoled if they don't see some sort of organization for events of the day.

When four-year-old Blake started vacation Bible school for the first time, he panicked at the rotating schedule that left him not knowing what was coming next. He explained to his mother, "Mommy, I don't know *when* we do anything!"

Only when his mother obtained a copy of the schedule for the rest of the week and carefully explained it to him, did Blake begin to calm down. He sighed a huge sigh of relief and said, "Oh yes, this is a *great* schedule." Even though he couldn't yet read, Blake clutched the schedule tightly in his little hands throughout the rest of the week. All was right in his Melancholy world, for he had a schedule!

Physical Awareness

Perfect Melancholy children are usually very much in tune with how they feel both emotionally and physically. They tend to focus their worries and hurts on their health and body pains. They need to let others know even their smallest concerns, often in the most dramatic fashion.

At Sunday school Melancholy Johnny was learning about how God created everything, including human beings. Little Johnny seemed especially intent when he heard how Eve was created out of one of Adam's ribs. Later in the week his mother noticed him lying down as though he were ill and asked, "Johnny, what's the matter?" Johnny responded, "I have a pain in my side. I think I'm going to have a wife."

Though she was amused by her son's expression of his physical ailment, Johnny's mother recognized her son's genuine concern over the discomfort he felt and his worry about its cause. Melancholy children need to know when they share their "problems" with their parents that they will not be ridiculed or dismissed as "worry warts." Often all they need is someone to listen and nod in quiet understanding as they list their little lamentations.

Not Peculiar

Melancholy children will greatly benefit from your understanding of their personality. At some time or other most of us have been told that we are strange, loud, weird, sullen, stupid, shy, bossy, depressed, or lazy. Melancholy personalities, the most introspective of all, take these remarks seriously and tend to feel there is something wrong with them.

More than any other, the Melancholy child is sensitive to the fact that she is different from others in many areas. It will be a great relief to this child to know that she isn't peculiar. Help your child celebrate the strengths of her personality rather than worry about its oddities.

Tender Hearts

If you listen carefully to some Melancholy children's stories, they will reveal a deeply tender heart. Sanguine children need love and affection too, but once their little love tanks are filled, they will quickly slip outdoors to seek the next fun adventure. Melancholy children tend to form deeper and longer-lasting attachments.

My friend Jeannie, a retired teacher, did some baby-sitting for a local family. The family's little boy, William, is a loving Melancholy who always appreciated Jeannie's soft touch and dedicated care of him. As he grew, the family didn't need Jeannie as much, so she hadn't seen sweet William for a year when a family death meant the parents had to go out of town. They called Jeannie to help, and when William heard she was coming, he said, "My heart is mended." When Jeannie arrived he explained, "My heart has been broken without you, but now it's all put back together again."

Jeannie recognizes the significance of her position as a heart mender: "There's a spiritual lesson here, for that's what the Lord does when we ask him in; he mends our broken hearts. I am more than willing to give William a vision of the Lord in me." Reach out to touch the hearts of your Melancholy children.

The thoughtful, deliberate nature of the Melancholy child can add rich depth to the character of your family. But, depending on your personality as a parent, you may find yourself struggling to connect with her. Understanding your differences will help you on your way to a meaningful relationship with this serious and sincere child.

eight

PARENTING YOUR MELANCHOLY CHILD

Your Perfect Melancholy children are the soul, mind, spirit, and heart of humanity. They help others around them to see beneath the surface of life. Their sense of detail and love of analysis propel them to high achievements, and their sensitive spirits make them compassionate toward the hurting.

This child's deep, thoughtful mind and analytical nature will carry him far, but taken to the extreme, these traits cause the Melancholy to brood over problems and constantly criticize everyone and everything that doesn't meet a perfect standard. As a parent, you must help your child capitalize on his Melancholy strengths while learning to cope with the less-than-perfect world around him.

Popular Parent with a Perfect Child

Although the Sanguine and Melancholy personalities are opposites, these two can share a complementary relationship if they work at understanding each other. Don't expect this child to be as demonstrative or bubbly as you, and learn to appreciate his quiet, reflective demeanor. Recognize that your child will have a different outlook on life than you, and take time to listen to his perspective.

Don't Cheer Me Up

The Popular parent or grandparent has to accept the Perfect child as he is and not try to make him over or cheer him up. When my grandson Randy was eight years old, I took him out for lunch and he ordered a hamburger. We sat down with our food and he took the top off his burger. He looked up with a sad face and said, "Do you know what I don't like about this place, Grammie?" I didn't think we'd been there long enough to give a review, but I dutifully asked, "What?"

"They don't even center the hamburger on the roll! All they do is throw down a roll, drop the burger on any old way, plop on two pickles and this lettuce leaf," he said with a sigh of disbelief, then added, "and they call this a hamburger!" He looked so depressed!

After explaining his disappointment to me, Randy centered his hamburger on the roll, took off the pickles, and ate his meal in a resigned fashion. When he had finished, he began to tell me how difficult it was living with his little Sanguine brother, Jonathan. "He sneaks into my room when I'm not around, he takes my toys out of the boxes and doesn't return them, and he steals my batteries."

As I tried to commiserate, he brightened up and said, "There's one good thing about having my new little brother, Bryan. Now Jonathan's going to find out what it's like to have a little brother." His glee soon turned to horror as he added, "I just realized, if Jonathan has a little brother that means I have two of them!" This thought so did him in that he could hardly get enough energy to walk to the car!

If I didn't understand the personalities, I would have felt our luncheon was a failure but the fact that I had listened and not tried to jolly him up gave him a feeling of acceptance. When I dropped him off at home, he thanked me for a "very nice time."

Conversation Starters

Not only do Sanguine parents have to learn to be good listeners, they must also learn how to draw out the Melancholy. Sandy had read a list of questions to ask your kids that would prompt discussion and let you know what they were really thinking and feeling. These questions included "What things do you really enjoy doing?" and "What makes you afraid?" Sandy tried them out on her Sanguine daughter Brie-Anne and the pair had a great conversation. Pleased with the outcome, Sandy tried the same questions with her Melancholy son Tayler. When she asked him what things he really enjoyed doing, he told her a few things such as reading and playing the piano. When she asked him what kinds of things made him afraid, he pondered for a while and then said, "That's really a good question." To this day he has not answered it. Sandy will have to work extra hard to get a response to that question out of her son!

When dealing with a Melancholy child, Sanguine parents really need to lower their expectations as to the amount of conversation and the enthusiasm over the questions. And parents must listen carefully when their Melancholy child does decide to communicate. If the child wants to talk, sit down and listen.

Everything's Fine

Despite a Sanguine parent's desire to hear every detail of a child's day, the Melancholy child isn't easily persuaded to join in a lively conversation about the day's events. If pushed too hard, the child may retreat and decide not to participate at all. A gentle and patient approach works best.

When her daughter Sharon was in preschool, Sally would pick her up at the end of the day and ask, "Hi, honey, how was your day?" Little Sharon would then proceed to entertain her mother all the way home, telling her all the wonderful events that had taken place that day. When her Melancholy son Scottie was in preschool, it was quite a shock for Sharon to get a much different answer to the same question. When asked about his day, Scottie would quietly say that it was "fine" (*fine* is a popular word for the Melancholy). To try to get the conversation going Sharon would prod, "Tell me what you did today." Scottie would sigh in response, then, while looking out the window of the car, he would say, "I dunno, Mom. I just want to think." As a Sanguine mother who loves conversation, Sally had to learn that silence was all she was going to get from him. Only when he was ready would he tell her if there was anything he deemed worth telling.

Even if they don't join in the fun of the moment, Melancholy children do want their Sanguine parents to be there with open ears and hearts to listen to and love them . . . when they are ready. You just need to be patient and wait for answers to come on *their* time. The more you push, the more reticent they become.

Give Me Some Space

Melancholies are by nature physically reserved and distant until they know or trust you. If they sense any disregard for their feelings they will withdraw not only emotionally but also physically. They protect their "personal space."

One of Tayler and Brie-Anne's major conflicts is in the area of affection. Ever since Tayler was a baby, Brie-Anne could not resist hugging her brother all the time. Tayler tolerated it for the most part when he was little, but as they have grown it is a different story. Tayler loves to be hugged by his parents but not by

Brie-Anne. Despite the rule that she isn't to hug Tayler because it bugs him so much, Brie-Anne can't resist trying. It's impossible for her to grasp that Melancholies are fussy about who they let into their personal space.

If you're a Sanguine parent, you may have to accept that your Melancholy child will be happier with a gentle pat on the back than with the big bear hug you'd like to give.

That's Not Funny

Popular parents may also struggle with Melancholy children who don't respond well to their bubbling humor. Since response is what Popular parents need, deeply intuitive Melancholies may make a decision not to give them what they want. They take secret pleasure in their quiet power to unnerve the parent with such a refusal. My Melancholy son once said, "It's amazing that people pay money to hear you talk! I guess that's because they don't have to listen to you for nothing." If I didn't know the difference between our personalities, I would have only tried harder to impress him with my humor. But instead, I was able to recognize that no matter how funny most people found me to be, my son wasn't likely to double over with laughter any time soon!

Please Don't Embarrass Me!

Not only does the Perfect child not appreciate the humor of the Popular parent, but because he takes everything to heart, he is easily hurt by the parent's flip comments that were intended to be funny.

Much to a Sanguine parent's chagrin, her Melancholy children may be embarrassed by her natural flair for fun and will dread whatever may come next. When your children are little, they'll probably think their Sanguine parent is a lot of fun. Hide-

and-seek games, songs and dances, pantomimes, and sketches entertain all personalities in the early years. But the Melancholy's positive response to high-energy theatrics begins to wane as the teen years approach. At that point, Melancholies may become downright embarrassed when a parent wears a T-shirt with sequins or smiles at a stranger.

One day my Melancholy son asked a favor of me. "When Mike's mother comes to pick him up, would you stay in the kitchen?" Puzzled, I asked why. "You'd be too much for her," he responded. Still not understanding his concern, I probed, "What do you mean?" "You'd intimidate her," he explained. Immediately I tried to reassure him. "I'll be good. I'll be quiet. I'll wear a black dress. I'll pretend I'm a plant." "See, that's what I mean. You'll do something strange." Fred shook his head. "Can't you just be normal?"

If you are a Sanguine parent, be sensitive to when each child turns from thinking you are amusing to seeing you as a family embarrassment.

On Time, Every Time

The Sanguine parent and Melancholy child have opposite concepts of time. The child's mental clock-calendar keeps him on time while recording the failures of the parent who doesn't know what day it is and has no sense of timing. I'm convinced that if a child prodigy were born to a Sanguine mother, the child's talent would die on the vine because the mother would forget to get him to his lessons and not have the discipline to sit by his side during hours of practice. That just wouldn't be much fun.

Even when the Sanguine parent *is* thinking about schedules and time, she still isn't completely on the same wavelength as the Melancholy child. Sanguine Suzy had assigned Melancholy son Ken to read each night for twenty minutes, a figure she had pulled out of the air. Ken had made himself a neat chart and each night he wrote down how many minutes he had read.

One night he approached her with a puzzled look on his face. As he pointed to his watch, he said, "Mom, I read twenty-four minutes and eighteen seconds, but I think it might have taken me a minute to find my book. I don't want to lie; so what should I put on my chart?"

Suzy wanted to laugh, but being sensitive to his serious nature, she said, "Honey, just write down twenty-five minutes."

"No, Mom," Ken said. "I'm not sure. It might have taken me longer to find my book. So how do I know exactly how long I read?"

Suzy couldn't believe he really cared about the seconds. As a typical Sanguine, she rounded everything up in her favor, never worrying about the exact numbers. But recognizing her son's precise nature, she suggested, "Why don't you round it down to twenty minutes just to be sure."

Ken left feeling much better about rounding the minutes down and knowing he hadn't taken more credit than he was due.

When parents understand the differences, they can handle each child according to his nature instead of laughing at him or making him feel stupid.

You Don't Have to Talk

Don't expect your Melancholy child to be as outgoing as you are. Speaker and author Bill Sanders learned that when he came to one of our seminars. His daughter Emily was four years old at the time and was a Perfect Melancholy. The night before the seminar Bill had given Emily an ultimatum: If she wouldn't answer people when they talked to her, he wouldn't take her with him to public places anymore. After learning about the personalities, Bill talked again with his daughter. "Guess what Daddy learned today, Emily," he encouraged her. "You can be anyone you want to be. You don't have to talk like Mom and Dad. If you don't want to say good-bye or hello, you don't have to." Her eyes brightened up and she hugged him, saying, "Oh, thank you, Daddy. I love you so much."

When you affirm your child's right to be less outgoing than you are, he will appreciate your encouragement more than you might expect!

No Surprises

Melancholies are most comfortable when going down a familiar path. They don't like surprises or unexplained roadblocks. Melancholy Keith was doing his homework with his Sanguine mother as his helper. He looked sad and soon began to cry. His assignment was to write five sentences about himself. He had already written five when he came to the word *etc.* "I don't know if I have one of these or not," he cried. "One of what?" his mother asked. "One of these," he said, pointing to the three letters.

"You don't have to have one. It just means that you can write other things about yourself," his mother explained. "But it doesn't say that," Keith moaned. "How do I know you are right?" Only when Keith's Melancholy father was called in to explain that *etc.* is an abbreviation for the word *plus,* did Keith relax. "Why didn't they just say so?"

Need to Know

Sanguine parents of organized Melancholy children can learn a tip or two about documenting details, checking off charts, and setting up schedules. A daily, weekly, or monthly schedule gives the Melancholy child a sense of security. From the time Melancholy Matthew was little, he has needed to have his clothes laid out at night for the next day. When he visits his grandmother, he calls ahead for the complete schedule so he knows what to bring. He arrives at breakfast with paper and pencil and asks to have a more detailed schedule of the day so he can get his activities in order. Because his grandmother understands the personalities, she humors him. She says it's even disciplined her a little to have him visit.

As a Sanguine parent you may think you don't need schedules, or that you can easily keep it all in your head. But try to be sensitive to your Melancholy child's need to know what's going to happen, when, and where. At the next *Nutcracker* performance, let your Melancholy child purchase a program. On the next family vacation, let him read the road map.

Too often our response to "Mom, where are we going?" or "Dad, how much longer until we get there?" is to tell the children to just be quiet and get in the car. When we dismiss their concerns, however, we can send them into depression or despair. Acknowledging their need for that sense of security eliminates their anxiety.

Less-than-Perfect Is Okay

Sanguine parents can help their intense Melancholy children relax by relating their own humorous stories of imperfection. It may not seem your child appreciates your stories, but they'll help him see that it's not the end of the world when something doesn't work or when something unexpected happens.

By sharing situations where she is not "perfect," Suzy helps her son Keegan learn that it's okay to relax. The other day Suzy left the kids' tennis rackets on top of the car and sped off to school. When she realized they were missing she retraced her route until she found them safe in the gutter. Suzy wants Keegan to know that everyone makes blunders and that even though she is sometimes frustrated by such silly mistakes, tomorrow is another day.

Although your Melancholy children may not laugh at your stories and may still go through life holding a higher standard for themselves, they will learn that less-than-perfect is okay.

Powerful Parent with a Perfect Child

The Powerful parent can motivate the reticent Perfect child who has so much ability. Choleric parents can stimulate the Melancholy's creativity and pull him out of his shell. But don't insist on quick, decisive action from this child who may want to mull things over for a while. And avoid spouting off critical or angry words that devastate your child. Speak softly and don't even carry a big stick. The controlling parent dealing with the sensitive child must aim to lift up the spirit of this little one and not crush it by her decisive action and quick answers.

Practical Sensitivity

Pragmatism can prevent a Choleric parent from seeing a situation through the sensitive eyes of the Melancholy child. When our grandson Randy had his fifth birthday, I had an all-purpose party for him, his father, and my husband—all of whom have February birthdays. Being practical and home very seldom, I felt this collective party was an admirable idea. Lauren and I thought we were killing three birds with one stone and were delighted with the pile of presents we had amassed for the occasion. In the middle of dinner, young Randy said he felt sick and withdrew to the bedroom. We finally pulled him out to open his presents, which he did mechanically with no enthusiasm. We pleaded with him to tell us what was wrong, but in typical Melancholy fashion, he would give us no clues.

Several days later, after much questioning, Lauren finally found out that he didn't want to have a party for everyone at one time. "That is worse than no party at all," he cried. He also was crushed when he realized the pile of presents was not all for him but had to be shared. "It's not fair to put the presents out there and then tell me they're not all mine," he complained. This double shock to his sensitive spirit had caused him to withdraw from his own party and kept him from enjoying the presents he received.

Try to be sensitive to your child's perspective. What you consider to be efficient and practical may make your child feel he isn't special or loved.

Love Them—Don't Lecture Them

If they don't take time to think through a child's response, Powerful parents are apt to lecture their Melancholy children for the attitudes they appear to see on the surface. It would have been easy for Lauren to lecture Randy on the evils of selfishness, but what he needed was a loving, soothing balm of understanding for his disappointment.

The Melancholy child will often come to conclusions about his wrong attitudes without a demeaning address from the parent. He will rethink his various experiences and ultimately come up with the "right" solution. Two years after the fateful joint birthday party, Randy approached me and said, "Grammie, it's all right if you have a party for everybody together. I'm grown-up now and I'm not selfish anymore."

If you are a Powerful parent with a Perfect child, tone down your approach, be sensitive to his feelings, and know that, like elephants, such children never forget.

Check the Facts First

Unlike Sanguines who will broadcast their every thought to whoever will listen, Melancholy children tend to protect their feelings by keeping them inside. Melancholy Joey came home with an excellent report card but he had flunked P.E. His Choleric father was furious. After a tirade that left his son in tears, Joey's mother sat down with him and said, "Tell me why you got marked down in P.E." Joey answered, "We have to take all our clothes off in front of the others and they make fun of me and say I'm fat. I won't undress, so I flunked."

If you see your Melancholy child struggling with his emotions, take the time to ask for an explanation or more details. Choleric parents can be too quick to judge; check the facts before you respond to you children.

Help *Not* Wanted

Don't assume that your child needs your help just because he doesn't appear to be making progress toward a goal.

Melanie was attending a wedding reception with her Melancholy son Charlie. After standing in the wedding cake line for quite a while, Melanie couldn't take any more time, so she told Charlie to wait in line, get his cake, and meet her at the car. After sitting impatiently in the car for several minutes, Melanie decided to check on Charlie. She figured that the adults had probably politely pushed her well-mannered son to the side and that he needed her help to get his piece of cake. Melanie determinedly walked up to Charlie, who was still in the same place in the line, and asked, "Charlie, did the adults get ahead of you? Let Mom get your cake for you." Without waiting for an answer, she charged ahead and got the cake.

When they got in the car, Melanie expected Charlie to be grateful for her help. Instead, he looked sad and as they drove away, he said, "Mom, I was waiting for the corner piece with all the frosting. I had counted pieces of cake and people in line and let other people ahead of me so it would come out right." Melancholy Charlie had quietly and strategically positioned himself to get what he wanted. And his mother's "help" had ruined his plan!

Stop to hear your child's plan before you plunge in to "help."

Encourage Assertiveness

After you learn to slow down and stop pushing your child, encourage him to speak up and politely make his needs known. You don't need to allow your child to be overlooked by others. Explain to him that others will push him around when he clams up and doesn't assert himself. Teach your child helpful phrases such as, "With all due respect" or "May I please explain?" These communication skills learned early in life will prepare your children to deal with insensitive friends and strangers and keep them from feeling downtrodden and picked on.

Take Time to Listen

Melancholy children may tend to keep many of their deep feelings inside, but when they are ready to share, they need a parent who will give them time and will pay attention to all their details. Joy's Melancholy grandson has a Choleric mother who has worn him out with her constant work assignments. She's hard on him and has no time as a single mother to hear his heart. Joy has become his listener. Last summer he went to a Christian camp and began serious Bible study. Once a week he calls his grandmother with a "word of wisdom." What a valuable friend he has in his grandmother!

If you're a Choleric parent to a sensitive Melancholy child, make sure you take the time to stop your busy schedule and listen. When your Melancholy child feels like talking, don't impatiently cut the conversation short. Hear him out to the end or he will shut down, draw more deeply inside, and become depressed.

An extra five or ten minutes of your time can make all the difference in meeting this child's emotional needs.

A Little Too Insightful?

Melancholy children, especially those who are older or in their teens, can have deep insight into their parent's personalities, especially their weaknesses. This can bother a Choleric parent who always wants to be in control or be right.

Andy had been struggling through a pretty serious case of teenage depression. Being the concerned mother that she is, Patricia had been trying to "talk things out" with him. Their "talking" turned into very loud and very emotional yelling. During the same few days when she was fighting with Andy, Patricia had a crash-and-burn disagreement with her best friend and was refusing to talk to her. Andy cut Patricia to the core with his observation of the situation. "Mom, do you know what your problem is? You are trying to communicate with a noncommunicator and not communicate with a communicator," the sixteen-year-old pointed out.

Choeric parents, can you tolerate some critical insight from your children? Never tolerate personal attacks, dishonor, or disrespect but do encourage your Melancholy children by thanking them for their valuable opinions.

Perfect Parent **with a** Perfect Child

The Perfect parent and Perfect child can make the best possible combination. With their mutual and deep artistic talent and exceptional organizational skills, they can accomplish a lot as they work together. And since they both value schedules, they're sure to get things done on time! Still, this pair will have their ups and downs.

Child Prodigies

When both parent and child are Perfect Melancholies, everything is done "in good order." Rooms are neat, charts are checked, and homework is completed on time. Child prodigies blossom in this environment where both parent and child are dedicated to intellectual pursuits and neither minds if practice is boring or the routine dull, as long as the goal is a worthy one. The Perfect parent recognizes the child's exceptional ability and will take time to patiently develop it.

Not every Melancholy child will be a genius, but if he is, the Perfect parent will be the most likely to spot the child's aptitude.

Shared Sensitivity

Because this parent and child share the same sensitivity, they will also share a sympathy with each other that no other combination can understand. But since they both get hurt easily, if one senses any opposition from the other, he or she may withdraw and get depressed instead of speaking up.

Perfect parents must guard against becoming depressed when their own adult world is not running smoothly. If they get too wrapped up in themselves, their children will feel neglected and become depressed. Two depressed Melancholies don't make for a happy family! It only takes a moment to reassure your Melancholy child that, although life is not perfect, your love for him is!

My Right Way, Not Yours

Although Melancholy children are basically neat, they want to be neat in their own way, and when this way conflicts with mother's way, they may go through a sloppy phase that belies their true personality. One reason may be a temporary rebellion. A teen boy told me that the only way to "really get to" his mother was to leave his room a mess each day. His mother's teary reaction gave him a feeling of control. Once he'd flexed his independent muscles, he went back to his neat ways with a feeling of self-satisfaction.

A naturally Melancholy child might also become sloppy if the parent's standards are so impossibly high that the child gives up on the whole program. Becky said, "No matter how hard I tried, my mother was never pleased and always told me I could do better. So one day I said to myself, 'Why are you killing yourself cleaning this room all the time when you can't make her happy anyway? Forget it!'"

One of the hardest lessons for the Perfect parent to learn is to keep the standards within reasonable reach. Help the child attain the goals and praise him when he does it correctly. Don't keep moving the target the minute he gets close to a bull's-eye.

Punishment That Fits the Crime

Melancholy parents sometimes see their children's faults and failures as more serious than they really are. When that happens, the corresponding discipline may be too intense for the situation, causing more emotional hurt than correction. On Melancholy Sally's eleventh birthday her parents promised her a party. That morning her twelve-year-old neighbor Doug asked her to come over and see his new BB gun. Sally was dying to see the gun but knew her Melancholy parents had forbidden her to visit when Doug's parents weren't home. Still, Sally went anyway, just for a quick peek. She didn't know that her dad had seen her through their living room window. When she came home, her parents spanked her and sent her to her room. Sally still recalls the hurt of that day. The spanking and going to her room would have been enough of a punishment, but her parents went a step further. They made her stay in all day and night, and they called her friends to cancel the birthday party. Sally didn't even get her presents for over a week. That wounded her spirit so deeply that she forgot all about what she had done wrong and focused instead on how her parents had hurt her.

It is important to teach your children values and to have them deeply instilled, but be careful that in your zeal and intensity to correct them, you don't overpunish and cause resentment. If you're not careful, you'll risk creating a deep well of resentment. Sally is forty today, and she still remembers the unjust punishment and cancellation of her eleventh birthday party.

Occupied for Hours

Where a Sanguine or Choleric child may be too impatient, Melancholy parents will be able to share their love for hobbies, artistic projects, or details with their Melancholy children. Rose's Melancholy husband and stepson like to spend Saturday mornings doing yard work. Rose used to stand at the kitchen window with her coffee and watch the two of them cutting the grass. Tom liked to do it perfectly and so did his son, Mike. They set up a little system of mowing and picking up the cuttings so that there was no mess. Tom taught Mike to cut the grass "stadium style," with perfect crisscrossed patterns in it. It took them twice as long as it would have otherwise, but they loved the result. Though Rose couldn't fathom spending so much time on such a task herself, she knew the activity was great father-son bonding time that allowed them to share their need for artistic perfection.

If you're a Melancholy parent with a Melancholy child, enjoy spending hours together working on detailed projects. But don't forget the rest of the chores and get the Cholerics in the family all upset.

Forever in Their Hearts

Melancholy children deeply enjoy their relationships with understanding Melancholy adults. Even Melancholy grandparents, aunts, and uncles can help fill the emotional needs of a tender-hearted Melancholy child. Nine-year-old Johannah was torn between sadness and expectancy at the prospect of moving with her family from Southern California to Ohio. On the last day before they left town, she and her Melancholy grandmother took a long walk, talked in depth, and then spent the last hour drawing pictures for each other as keepsakes.

When Johannah finished her picture, she handed her grandmother a self-portrait then said in profound Melancholy fashion, "Good people are never forgotten. I won't forget you. Don't forget me. Sunshine can only be seen in the light. Let it shine!" Deeply moved and in tears, Grandmother planned a trip to Ohio on the spot.

If you are the Melancholy parent of a Melancholy child, you'll probably find it easy to relate to your sensitive child. You may be tempted to go to the ends of the earth for this child's affection and loyalty, but it's often not necessary. Remember that once you're in the heart of a Melancholy child, you're likely to stay there forever.

Peaceful Parent with a Perfect Child

Neither the Phlegmatic parent nor the Melancholy child needs a lot of "chatter," so these natural introverts enjoy just being in each other's company. Unfortunately, because neither of them tends to initiate conversations, this quiet company can breed a severe lack of communication unless the parent takes the initiative to draw out the child at some point.

Communication Shutdown

When the moody Melancholy withdraws and becomes depressed the Peaceful parent usually prefers not to deal with the problem. It's easier to avoid it and hope it goes away. One Peaceful father said of his Melancholy child, "When he clams up, it takes too much effort to find out what's wrong. I give him a couple of chances, and if he doesn't tell me, then I figure it's his problem." This father is right about the situation being a problem. If the child believes his father doesn't care, he will retreat further. By the time he's a teen, the two of them will have no communication at all. The Perfect child needs a parent who is willing to dig deeply—all the way, all the time—and sit patiently with him until he finally opens up. Enjoy quiet time with your child, but don't give up trying to get him to open up to you. It will be worth the effort.

Quiet Interests

As we've noted, the Peaceful parent and Perfect child can enjoy each other's company without having to say a word. Neither needs to go anywhere or do anything exciting; they both enjoy silence and lack of conflict. Their quiet interests complement each other well.

Perfect Serena and her Peaceful mother used to spend hours sewing together in silence. Serena's need for perfect top stitching was a delight to her mother who didn't have to take any extra time or effort ripping out or redoing seams for her daughter. Peaceful parents should look for mutual interests they can develop with their child. When they do, they'll find great satisfaction in working together.

Time to Get Moving

Although they work well together, the introspective Melancholy and the unmotivated Phlegmatic may have a hard time setting challenging goals. Both of them need to be inspired to get down to work, and they too easily settle for the status quo, saying, "Tomorrow is another day." A child with just a hint of Choleric initiative may become critical of the Peaceful parent and decide it's time to impose Melancholy organization and motivation. When a parent resists, the child may pull back and quit trying to communicate altogether. If you're a Peaceful parent, don't make your Melancholy child motivate you. Perk yourself up and take some initiative or the division between you and your child may grow beyond repair.

Regardless of your personality as a parent, remember to give your Melancholy children plenty of love and support. Compliment them sincerely and lovingly to reinforce your appreciation of them. Accept their quiet composure and quest for solitude, and allow your Melancholy children to spend some quiet time alone. But make sure they don't become antisocial in the process. With your direction, your meticulous Melancholy will become a serious, sensitive individual on the path to success.

nine

PRACTICES OF A PLEASANT PHLEGMATIC

PHLEGMATIC

Peaceful Personality
The Introvert • The Follower • The Pessimist

Emotional needs: peace and relaxation, attention, praise, self-worth, loving motivation

Avoids: conflict, confrontation, initiative, decisions, extra work, responsibility, tension, quarrels

Strengths	Weaknesses
BABY	
• serious	• guarded
• easygoing	• unresponsive
• undemanding	• slow
• happy	• shy
• adjustable	• indifferent
• loves naps	

Strengths	Weaknesses
CHILD	
• watches others	• selfish
• easily amused	• teasing
• little trouble	• avoids work
• dependable	• fearful
• lovable	• quietly stubborn
• agreeable	• lazy
TEEN	
• pleasing personality	• quietly stubborn
• witty	• indecisive
• good listener	• unenthusiastic
• mediates problems	• too compromising
• hides emotions	• unmotivated
• leads when pushed	• sarcastic
• casual attitude	• uninvolved
	• procrastinates

A mother was preparing pancakes for her sons, Choleric Kevin and Phlegmatic Phil. The boys began to argue over who would get the first pancake, so their mother decided to teach them a moral lesson. "If Jesus was sitting here, he'd say, 'Let my brother have the first pancake. I can wait.'"

Choleric Kevin turned to his brother and quickly directed, "Phil, you be Jesus." Phil agreed!

The Phlegmatic child is the easiest and least demanding of all. While the Sanguine is screaming for attention, the Melancholy is not willing to tell you why he is depressed, and the Choleric is yelling, "Hey, give me some credit!" the Phlegmatic is quietly watching the family parade as if it were a TV sitcom. The Phlegmatic has nothing she feels compelled to do, and even if everyone else does nothing too, she will still be content. It's easy to ignore the Phlegmatic, but just because this child doesn't demand attention doesn't mean she doesn't have any needs.

Quiet Needs

Phlegmatics have a low energy level; they hate conflict and confrontation and crave *peace and quiet.* They will love you forever if you fight their battles and relieve them from stress. Though this child lacks an internal drive to accomplish something, you can move her to action with *loving motivation* from you.

Even though the Phlegmatic child doesn't compete for *attention* or *praise,* especially in a highly motivated family, she needs both. In their absence she will grow up with a low sense of *self-worth.* This child's emotional needs are rather low-key, but if you don't meet them, she will feel insecure and will never achieve her potential. Phlegmatics need you to tell them you love and respect them for who they are, not for how much they do.

It's easy for this child to slip through the cracks and be ignored. When that happens, she grows up with little self-respect, believing that nobody cares. Take time from the demanding children to let your Phlegmatic know how much you care for her. And make sure you don't tie love to accomplishment. Instead, compliment this child's sweet spirit and concern for people in need.

Open Up Options

Phlegmatics are usually single-interest children, and it's the parent's job to find out what it is that will excite and motivate this child. Groupies hung around the stage door waiting for Alene's Phlegmatic son Eric. A talented drummer, Eric was a great musician with good stage presence. While his parents were supportive, his desire for a career with a rock band concerned them. After high school graduation Eric worked in a fish market and played sporadic gigs on weekends. He was content. Two years went by and all his parents' suggestions about education fell on deaf ears. They knew they couldn't push him into a different life, but they did want him to choose a different goal in life.

Simultaneously Eric's sister, two years older, had just finished a program at Ohio State and won a semester in Switzerland working for a poster company. Laura's work/education opportunity there proved to be a wonderful experience. But even with all the adventure of her job and new little apartment, she soon became homesick.

With the hope that a visit from her brother would help with the homesickness and also motivate him, Eric's parents approached him about traveling to Switzerland. He was challenged to travel that distance on his own but agreed, and the ticket was acquired. Eric spent two weeks with Laura; it was an opportunity of a lifetime and turned out to be a life-changing experience for him.

When Eric arrived home, without a word, he made an appointment to get a physical exam, registered at the local college, and cut his hair, inch by inch. He continued to play with the band and work in the fish market, but he also aggressively sought a career. Today Eric is a graduate of a four-year college and works as a nurse with children who have been severely burned. His ambition is to go on a mercy trip to South America or Africa and plans are underway to make that happen.

Eric recalls that he was shocked into reality when he saw his sister getting paid to work, live, and vacation in Switzerland while anticipating a job in the United States, just because she had an education, was using her talents, and had set some goals beyond the moment.

Helping the Phlegmatic by showing her options is more effective than nagging her to get moving. As the parent, don't give up trying different possibilities. Sooner or later you'll hit on something that will really excite her.

Always the Easy Way

Peaceful children have an innate desire to find the easy way to do anything. They look carefully at any project and slowly choose the path of least resistance.

Shirley's granddaughter Lindsay, a Phlegmatic all the way, was sitting at the computer playing a game of tic-tac-toe. She had to play the part of both competitors since there was no one else to play with at the moment. Shirley let her play for a while. Later as she walked past the computer, she noticed Lindsay was sitting there with her arms crossed—watching! When Shirley asked her what she was doing, Lindsay answered, "I figured out how to make the game play itself and now all I have to do is watch!"

Work as Discipline

Phlegmatic children like to avoid hard work, tedious work, or any work that doesn't fit their interests! Remember this when assigning chores as punishment. Rose told me about disciplining her Phlegmatic nephew.

Rose had sent her Choleric stepson, Mike, and his Phlegmatic cousin, Joe, off to do chores. It was late in the afternoon and the two nine-year-olds had not done one single assignment Rose had given them that morning, so she decided to separate them, have them finish their chores, and pile on even more mundane tasks as their discipline. "You *will* learn to finish your work before you play," she informed them. Rose was pleased with herself for coming up with a punishment that worked to her advantage by getting some extra work out of the kids in the process. When she heard Mike humming the theme from *Pink Panther,* though, she realized she wasn't as smart as she thought.

Bright-eyed and bouncing, Mike was perched up on the bathroom counter cheerfully wiping the mirrors. Choleric Mike didn't really mind the work, and when challenged, he put all his energy into doing it as fast as he could. In contrast, Joe sat on his knees, shoulders sagging, sad-faced, and depressed. As he wiped the coffee table in ver-r-r-y slow motion, he heard Rose come into the room, looked up, and whined, "Aunt Rosie, do I have to do all the tables?" Though the extra chores didn't work as effective discipline for Choleric Mike, they were making a big impression on Phlegmatic Joe!

Lists Aren't for Keeping

Phlegmatics find great satisfaction in relieving themselves of responsibility. A Peaceful daughter called her Choleric mother to give an exciting report. "Mom, I did the neatest thing today and I want to tell you about it!" she said. "With a legal pad and pen in hand, I walked around the entire house and made a long list of all the chores that needed attention. Then I sat down on the couch and simply tore up the list and trashed it! And I'm feeling good!"

Your Phlegmatic children may acknowledge things that need to be done in their lives, but their natural inclination will always be to tear up the list and trash it!

Can I Retire Yet?

Relaxing is a major goal for Peaceful children and one they still embrace as adults. While Cholerics would never dream of quitting work at any age, retirement is the Phlegmatic's dream! A Choleric wife told me how her Phlegmatic husband spent his whole life working at a job he didn't like because it was easier to stay than look for something new. He kept saying he was living each day waiting for retirement so he would never have to work again. Now he is retired and each morning he gets up, goes to his easy chair by the window, and watches the neighborhood people go to work. He smiles, sits awhile, and resumes his post when the workers start coming home. He says he's having the time of his life, but he's driving his wife crazy.

This retirement dream starts early for the Phlegmatic. Last summer Kim's parents lived with her for a month while their new house was being finished. They are both retired and enjoy a much slower pace of life than do Kim and her family. They must have made retirement look pretty good to Kim's ten-year-old son Brenden, because he proclaimed, "I can't wait until I retire!" As if he's had much of a life in his ten years to retire *from!* Don't be surprised if your Peaceful child wants to retire, even at age ten!

Born Ready . . . for Bed

Phlegmatics are so naturally relaxed that their favorite activity is often sleep. Ten-year-old Brenden constantly battles with his mother over his ultra-laid-back, easygoing temperament. It's very hard to get him motivated to do anything! Still, his Sanguine side keeps his family so entertained with jokes and smiles that it's hard to come down too hard on him. But even his humor has a Phlegmatic twist. His mother entered his room to tuck him in bed one night and asked, "Are you ready?" He replied, "I was born ready, Mom!" She probed further, asking, "Born ready for what?" and was met with a classic Phlegmatic response, "I was born ready for bed!" So true! Brenden was a great sleeper, even as a baby!

Ready to Give Up

If Phlegmatics don't see the point in what they're doing, they'll quickly give up. They assume the same is true of others. Phlegmatic Johnny watched, fascinated, as his mother smoothed cold cream on her face. "Why do you do that, Mommy?" he asked. "To make myself beautiful," she replied, then began removing the cream with a tissue. Seeing her action, Johnny piped up, "What's the matter? Giving up?"

Phlegmatic children figure that when you stop doing something, you've given up on reaching a goal. Make sure your Peaceful child doesn't get the impression you've given up on her!

Sweetness Cloaks a Will of Iron

When the right button is pushed, sweet, soft, Peaceful children will display a strong, stubborn will of iron. Phlegmatic Ashley was always a "carry me" child, while her stepsister Jessica, a strong Choleric, was the "put me down" child. Ashley wanted all of her mom's attention, and Jessica wanted to be left alone. Ashley was Miss Whatever and Jessica was Miss Perfection. But though Ashley seemed a lot more easygoing than Jessica, her will of iron occasionally reared its head. When Ashley decided she didn't want to do something, no amount of threatening would change her mind. Her parents tried every form of discipline. One day, after a long battle, Ashley's father told her to go to her room. In a quiet and calm voice she said, "No, I don't want to." So her dad physically picked her up, carried her down the hall, and put her in her room. As soon as he let go, she scrambled quickly out beneath his legs before he could turn around. He picked her up again and put her back in her room. She repeated her exit. The third time he put her farther into her room and beat her to the door, closing it and holding it tightly so she could not turn the knob. She screamed something unintelligible. A few minutes later the phone rang. The neighbor from across the street had just been gardening in her front yard and now had some advice for the frazzled parents. "You may want to consider shutting Ashley's bedroom window. She's hanging out of it screaming," the neighbor said, laughing. Ashley's parents ran outside to see her half-in and half-out of the window, yelling, "Somebody help me! They're killing me in here!"

Although Phlegmatic children will go along with the family program most of the time, be prepared for the times they won't. They will need as strong a boundary and as stiff a consequence as any Choleric child to get them back on track.

ten

PARENTING YOUR PHLEGMATIC CHILD

Phlegmatic children are the most enjoyable and easygoing people there are. They're almost always accommodating, incredibly patient, and easily pleased. But these relaxed kids lack the internal drive of the Melancholy and Choleric, so they need parents to help them set and achieve goals.

Peaceful children need constant reinforcement and encouragement to make the effort of working toward a goal worthwhile. Be sure to reward your young Phlegmatic for every achievement, however small. The light at the end of the tunnel will keep this child moving only if he receives encouragement along the way.

It's easy to view passive Peaceful children as incapable. They are content to let others help them and make their decisions, but that's not because they aren't able to do things for themselves. They simply choose the path of least resistance—and least work—in all situations. Teach your child to clearly evaluate options and make choices rather than always following the crowd. As he does so and begins to take responsibility for different areas in his life, you'll be amazed at how proficient your quiet Phlegmatic can be!

Popular Parent with a Peaceful Child

Sanguine parents will enjoy the relaxed, unpressured attitude of their Peaceful Phlegmatic children. In fact, they may enjoy it so much that they forget to work on disciplining themselves and their children to accomplish something! Phlegmatic children need to be motivated by loving encouragement and a good example. Though it's not their natural strength, Popular parents need to take the lead in demonstrating self-discipline for their children.

In the area of decision making these two are leagues apart. The Popular parent loves to do things on the spur of the moment, but the Peaceful child, who has difficulty making decisions in the best of times, becomes traumatized when an excited parent pushes for an instant decision ("Get ready! We've got two minutes before we have to leave.").

These two personalities differ the most in their level of enthusiasm. The Popular parent lives for excitement; the Peaceful child wants to avoid it. The Popular parent loves noise and confusion; the Peaceful child wants it quiet. To enjoy a healthy relationship this parent and child need to learn to understand and adapt to each other's preferences.

Turn Down the Volume

Popular parents have to understand that their friendly, outgoing nature comes across as loud and aggressive to their Peaceful children, and their sense of humor and spontaneous actions embarrass the more reticent nature. Without realizing this and turning down their volume, Sanguine parents can humiliate their Phlegmatic children and drive them into depression.

Fred Jr. didn't like to go marketing with me because I always spoke to absolute strangers whom he felt I had no business addressing. Before his track meets he would ask me not to cheer because hearing my voice unnerved him. All the other mothers were screaming, but I had to be restrained. Peaceful children want their parents' support; they just want them to be quiet about it.

Why Can't We Just Follow the Rules?

While rules rarely hold a creative Sanguine back, Phlegmatic children would much rather be inconvenienced than take a chance on being publicly reprimanded for breaking them. Popular Debbie and her children drove more than a hundred miles to get to the church where I was holding a seminar and arrived several hours before the scheduled time. Debbie hadn't sent for tickets ahead of time, assuming there would be no problem picking them up at the door. She walked into the empty church in the afternoon and put Bibles on front row seats to reserve them.

When she returned in the evening, she was given green pieces of construction paper cut in squares as tickets and told these tickets would allow her into the overflow room where she could watch on a monitor. Naturally she was not about to sit in an overflow room so she went to the entrance with her green tickets and told the lady at the door that she knew me and had already saved her seats in the auditorium. The woman wasn't impressed and responded, "You can pick up your Bibles afterwards. But you may not go in there now. To get in this room you need pink tickets, and those are sold out."

Debbie looked around and saw people passing in pink pieces of paper. Sensing she was going to do something strange, her children begged her to go sit where she belonged. But while they were tugging on her, she spotted a pink poster on the wall. Without hesitation she pulled the poster down and asked her son for his pocket knife. She took her Sanguine daughter to the ladies' room where they laid the poster on the counter and measured and cut out pink tickets to match their green ones. Some people looked at her strangely, but no one dared ask what she was doing.

Debbie threw her green tickets in the trash and emerged with pink ones as if she'd had them in her possession for weeks. Her other children had been quietly huddled in the foyer awaiting her return and wondering what mother was up to now. She smiled and told them proudly, "We have pink tickets. Let's go." She pushed them all to a different entrance, avoiding the lady who had refused to let her in. The person at this door took her pink tickets without question, and she proceeded to the front where her seats were awaiting her arrival. She was thrilled with her brilliant handling of the situation and didn't realize this whole procedure had made nervous wrecks of her children. Later, when she asked one Peaceful child how she'd enjoyed my speaking, the girl replied, "I didn't hear a word she said. I was scared to death any minute the police were going to come in and drag us away." What seems like high adventure to the Sanguine may strike terror in the heart of a Phlegmatic.

Creative or Humiliating?

Sanguine parents and Phlegmatic children share an appreciation of wit, but parents shouldn't be surprised if these children fail to get excited about some of their "brilliant" ideas. When this is the case, don't push for energetic enthusiasm. The more you do, the more stubborn your child will become.

Edie was trying to come up with a visual way to teach her study group the principle that looks can be deceiving and that we shouldn't make snap judgments about people. Inspiration struck her when her group moved for a night into the church's new youth center. Edie decided she would dress like a teen and see how many made snap judgments about her.

Sanguines never do things halfway, so Edie really got into the charade. She went to a resale shop and got teen clothes and a dog collar necklace with black nails sticking out of it. Her hairdresser gave her a purple rinse, then ratted and spiked her hair with gel. She suggested Edie buy white makeup and powder, blood-red lipstick and nails, and dark eye shadow. She also supplied her with paste-on ear dots and a transfer tattoo. By the time Edie was ready she was delighted with her results and decided to appear for dinner in her costume. She thought her husband and son would laugh along with her and praise her for her creativity. Instead, her Melancholy husband was shocked, could hardly eat, and wouldn't kiss her good-bye. Her Phlegmatic son was humiliated and proclaimed, "You're lucky I'm not getting sick all over this table!"

Edie learned not to pursue such a "creative" idea without first running it by the family. Even if you make a hit with your public, when you humiliate or embarrass your family, the venture isn't worth the price of the purple spiked hair and phony tattoo!

What Time Is It Anyway?

Sanguines and Phlegmatics are both casual about appointments and time. But the Sanguine's forgetfulness when it comes to time can sometimes cause scary situations for the Phlegmatic child. Sanguine Ellen loved to teach and took a job as a substitute teacher in a local district. She was home in time for her first grader's return and her younger children were able to attend a competent day care. One day she got out early from her assignment and, as only a Sanguine would do, she seized the moment to go shopping.

She found an exciting sale on children's clothing at a store where she rarely shopped but simply had to see what she could find. She was keeping careful tabs on her watch so as not to be late and was thankful to be getting so much done in such good time. Knowing she soon had to be on her way lest she not get there before Brett arrived, she drew her shopping spree to a close.

When Ellen got into her car she realized that her watch had stopped and that little Brett was due home at any moment. She prayed that the bus would arrive later than normal; it had done so a few times in the past. She hoped she'd be lucky and that today would be one of those times.

Her Sanguine mind flashed between thinking about what a deal she'd gotten on so many cute new clothes for the kids and the feeling that somehow she was in real trouble. Her car couldn't go fast enough. She looked at her watch for the eighth, ninth, and tenth times, then looked at the clock in the car.

Ellen sped to the baby-sitter to pick up her two youngest children, then rushed home to find that Phlegmatic Brett hadn't returned home yet. She was relieved . . . for a while. But as she realized that the bus had never been that late, her fragile calm quickly gave way to panic. She tried to think like her six-year-old. She had never discussed with Brett where he should go in such a circumstance. Where could he have gone? She looked everywhere—down at the water's edge, at the public dock, at the harbor police. But no luck!

It began to rain and the last brightness of the afternoon's sun was darkening as she headed home without him. She stood in the street and called Brett's name several times. Ellen was frantically trying to figure out where Brett could have gone and was preparing to phone in a lost child report when Brett came in the back door. He put his bags down but didn't talk to her. He wasn't the happy little guy who usually burst through the door and he resisted her hug as she screamed, "Where have you been?" After explaining that he had been at a neighbor down the street, Brett pulled away and retreated to his room.

Brett claims he doesn't remember the incident today, but Ellen surely does. She says that was the day she finally learned to keep track of time and not blame others for her mistakes.

Powerful Parent with a Peaceful Child

The Powerful Parent loves the Peaceful child because by nature he is a follower and is most willing to do what the Powerful parent instructs. Since this child's inner desire is to avoid any sign of conflict, he wants to do what will make the parent happy. This spirit of obedience pleases the Powerful parent who aims to keep people under control.

This combination is what we tend to think of as the "norm." We expect parents to be disciplined leaders who work lovingly with their obedient children. But the problem with this ideal blend comes in the Phlegmatic's lack of motivation. Because the Powerful parent is the most productive and thinks in units of work, she can't believe that people exist who have no burning desire to "get up and at 'em." She views people without goals as lazy and tends to look at the Peaceful child and wonder when he is going to get moving. The parent begins to ask questions about what the child will do, expecting her words to spur him to action. But she actually accomplishes the opposite. Because the Peaceful person's greatest emotional need is to feel valued, pointed questions convince the Phlegmatic child that he is unloved and cause him to shut down what little motivation previously existed.

Problems arise when the Powerful parent overwhelms the Peaceful child, can't understand why he lacks ambition, and knocks him down in an effort to get the child up and moving. Aggressive motivation doesn't work with the Phlegmatic; but a Powerful parent who understands a child's nature and makes him feel capable and valuable will become a hero to the child.

Use kind words to motivate this child but also create an atmosphere in which he can relax and have "down time."

You Decide

The agreeable Phlegmatic's desire for peace is difficult for opinionated Cholerics to understand. They think Phlegmatics must be faking their lack of concern for decision making. Cholerics care so much about everything that they can't believe Phlegmatics don't care at all.

A storekeeper held out two lollipops to two children. Choleric Mike grabbed the purple one he liked and gave the yellow one to Phlegmatic Matt. The boys' mother intervened, asking, "Matt, which one would you really like?" Matt responded in a typical Phlegmatic manner, "I would like to have whichever one he wants to give me."

John is a college sophomore with a Choleric sister at the same college. He is a sweet, dependable Phlegmatic who is happy for his sister to set up his social life. When his grandmother asked him what type of girlfriend he was looking for, he answered, "I'm not really looking for one, but it would have to be someone my sister would approve of." And she's probably out there interviewing candidates!

Whether young or old, Phlegmatics would rather leave the decision making to others. That way if it turns out to be wrong, they don't have to shoulder the blame.

What's the Point?

Even a young child notices when he is different from the rest of the family. If he's not affirmed for his own personality, the Phlegmatic child will tend to think there's something wrong with him. This is particularly true in a house full of Cholerics who run around setting and achieving goals and working around the clock, leaving the Phlegmatic feeling worthless in their dust.

Brenden is a superbright kid. He gets decent grades and he's in an accelerated program at school. But he's rather like the absentminded professor—he has an awful time remembering his responsibilities. Even with three Choleric family members around to remind him, he hasn't caught on to remembering what he's supposed to do. He has a checklist to fill in each week but he has to be reminded throughout the day to look at it and see what he should be doing.

One night at bedtime Kim was getting after Brenden for a couple of tasks that were uncompleted even after several reminders. She must have seemed pretty disappointed in him, because he got big tears in his eyes. When asked what was wrong, he said he wasn't sure he could explain it very well. He was quiet a minute, thinking what to say, and then with his hands covering his closed eyes, he simply said, "I'm pointless!" Kim really wasn't expecting such a despairing confession from her ten-year-old! But she dared not laugh. Instead, she asked what he meant, and he restated that his life had no point!

Kim tried to encourage him, saying, "Bren, you're ten! Your point is to go to school and learn stuff and just grow up!" His response was, "Life just doesn't seem to mean very much at all." Kim knew by this statement that her Phlegmatic son wasn't getting enough affirmation from the rest of the family. So after they talked things out that night, she and her husband made a renewed effort to affirm Brenden's character, even though his personality is completely different from the rest of the family. Everyone needs to feel they have a point!

In recent weeks Brenden has become involved with the chess club at school. (Isn't that a Phlegmatic pastime?) He's an excellent chess player and seems to have a natural ability. Last week when Kim asked Brenden how he was feeling about finding his "point" in life, he said, "I think my point could be chess!" He wants to start an after-school chess club, and Kim will encourage him to do so. He insists he doesn't want to be a professional chess "nerd," but he likes chess and now he has a point!

Take time to motivate your Phlegmatic child and help him find what he is good at in life. Don't let this child grow up saying, "I'm pointless."

Don't Do It for Them

Allowing a Phlegmatic child to function in his weaknesses through childhood can result in devastating effects in his adult life. Phlegmatic children who never learn to take responsibility for themselves will make poor marriage partners and even more pitiful parents.

Tim's parents allowed his older sisters to serve and care for their "little" brother well past his baby years. When he shook his iced tea glass at the table, the girls quickly rose to get him more. When he left his books on the table as he ran for the bus, they would scoop them up for him. Even after the children became adults, the girls still waited on their brother.

One afternoon Tim left his preschool-age son playing on the driveway in his parked car while he joined the rest of the men upstairs watching football. One of the in-laws drove up, saw the three-year-old behind the wheel of the car, which still had the keys in it, and came upstairs to tell Tim. He didn't move. After a few minutes someone else came up and complained about the danger of little Timothy playing in the car with the ignition keys in it. Finally, two others left the room to rescue Tim's son from the driveway. He still didn't see the problem and he never will as long as others are there to take care of things for him!

It may seem easier to do things *for* the Phlegmatic child than to wait for him to do them, but don't give in to the temptation. If the Phlegmatic child doesn't learn to take responsibility for tasks, he may never "grow up" and assume responsibility for his life. Help him get organized but don't do the work for him.

Consider *All* the Facts

The Peaceful's easygoing nature is often quite forgiving of others' oversights. And the Powerful parent, who is easily distracted by more demanding people and tasks, will probably need such forgiveness. But even when the Choleric parent should be grateful for a child's willingness to forgive and forget, this highly driven individual can quickly become impatient with the Phlegmatic child's laid-back approach to life.

Easygoing Phlegmatic Tommy had to stay after school for baseball practice and his Choleric dad was supposed to pick him up at four o'clock. When practice ended, the parking lot was full of parents picking up little players, but Tommy's dad wasn't one of them. Tommy soon tired of standing and decided to sit down on the hard concrete sidewalk. After a couple of minutes he looked over to the grassy area under a tree next to the parking lot and decided that would be a much more comfortable place to sit. A few minutes later Tommy realized it would be even more comfortable if he could lie down in the cool grass. So he squished his baseball mitt into a pillow, lay down, and fell into a deep sleep within minutes.

When Tommy woke, it was dark. He panicked because he knew his dad would be angry that he wasn't waiting where he was supposed to be. And he was hungry. When he walked to the church next door and asked if he could use the phone to call his parents, the pastor was relieved to see him. "Your dad came looking for you, and no one could find you, Tommy," he explained. "Your parents have been very worried and were thinking of calling the police!" Within a few minutes Tommy's dad drove up, Tommy climbed in the car, and they were on their way home.

If you were Tommy's Choleric parent, how would you react? Would you yell at him for not waiting out in the open or would you understand his need to lie down and relax after a long day at school and baseball practice? Would you realize that your own tendency to be late because there's always just one more task to be accomplished contributed to the situation? Would you admit that you drove quickly around the parking lot, impatiently scanned the scene, and took off determined that Tommy would learn a lesson? Choleric parents easily jump to wrong conclusions if they don't take time to analyze all the facts, including the different personalities of their children.

Tommy was grateful that his dad did understand both his own personality and that of his son. On their way home, his dad apologized for being late and suggested that in the future they should pick an exact place for Tommy to wait. Now that's a nice Choleric positive—acknowledging his own responsibility and looking for a solution at the same time!

Choose Your Battles

Consistent follow-through with discipline helps with Phlegmatics, but sometimes they still don't respond the way parents would like them to. And the more the Choleric parent pushes, the more likely the Phlegmatic child is to resist.

When Lucy first learned about the personalities, she finally understood why even the simplest activities always seemed to be difficult for her oldest son. When Jeremy was a preschooler, getting him dressed and in the car for school was a chronic battle. No matter how prepared they were the night before, he dawdled and drifted the morning away, even when Lucy used a timer and gave him an alarm clock. One night she told him they would leave for the thirty-minute ride to school at a certain time the next morning, whether he was ready or not.

As the departure time approached the next morning, Jeremy was still in his underwear, despite the timer's periodic warning.

When the time came to leave, Lucy got in the car with an immodest and very vocal Jeremy in his underwear. He couldn't believe his mother was actually taking him to school in this condition and asked, "What are you going to do? Leave me like this? I'm not going to get out of the car." Lucy had gathered his school clothes in a sack since she suspected those she had laid out for him to wear wouldn't find their way onto his body in time. So she nonchalantly replied, "It's up to you. I brought clothes in the car if you want them. They are in that sack. When we get to school, though, you are going in as you are."

By the time they arrived at the school, Jeremy had everything on but his shoes. Many subsequent days they left the house with Jeremy in his underwear, arriving at school with Jeremy still putting the finishing touches on his apparel. Things changed only when Jeremy, in his own sweet time, decided his effort was better spent dressing at home.

Jeremy and Lucy fought a similar battle over his room. The more she moaned over his mess, the more determined he was not to clean it. Jeremy's best friend invited him over to spend the night, and he went numerous times. When it was their turn to host and Jeremy wanted the family to invite Matt over for a night, Lucy told him it was a great idea . . . once he cleaned his room.

Five months went by, and Jeremy never cleaned up his room. Matt moved a thousand miles away, leaving Jeremy alone in his mess and Lucy still upset. Once Matt left town, Lucy cleaned Jeremy's room. Her only hope of motivating her son to action had disappeared!

Phlegmatic Jeremy simply refused to budge when his mother pushed him. As in the case of his preschool dressing habits, he couldn't be motivated by anyone other than himself. And in this case, he just didn't see the point in giving in.

Choleric parents will need to let some things go with their Phlegmatic children. Don't tolerate disrespect, dishonor, or deceit, and enforce appropriate standards for acceptable behavior at home and school. But learn to choose your battles or you'll never find a moment of peace to relieve your frustration with your child's habits!

Get Moving!

Parents need to understand a child's personality to discipline and motivate him effectively. When they don't, there's not much chance for a healthy, nurturing environment.

Al remembers spending countless hours alone in his room, writing pages of lines as punishment for misbehavior. All he wanted in life was to watch TV and have some fun doing it. Given his parents' high expectations, though, his low grades contributed to the financial well-being of the paper and pencil industries (countless pages of "I-must-do-my-homework-after-school" and "I-must-do-what-I-am-told" lines)! Rather than motivating him to put energy into his work, though, Al just concentrated on finding ways to conserve energy even while being punished. At one point he figured out how to use seven pencils at a time to record the countless lines of disciplinary sentences.

As long as he felt the disapproval of his parents, Al was unable to motivate himself to expend any effort to live up to their expectations. He was sure he would fail anyway. He needed to be loved and accepted for who he was before he would be motivated to step out and try something new.

When his high school years arrived, Al's friend talked him into going out for the soccer team. He played only about five minutes of the last game in the season that year, but the coach took a personal interest in him and insisted Al go to summer camp. That summer at camp Al found people who cared and could help him develop his skills. When he returned home, he began to spend six to eight hours a day practicing out in the ball field across from his house. Soccer became a huge motivator for him, and his mother was finally able to get her son up and moving. Al began to develop new respect for himself when he could see the improvement of his skill level, and the next season he returned as the leading scorer for the team. At last, this single-interest child had found a reason to do something!

Don't expect your Phlegmatic children to live up to *your* expectations in every area of life. Help them find their own areas of interest and set goals for success.

I'll Do It . . . on *My* Time

Choleric parents often become impatient when their Phlegmatic children don't develop as quickly as they've planned. Greg's Phlegmatic personality was obvious from the beginning. He was two weeks overdue; it was just too much work to be born! He never sat up, spoke, or took a step until one day, while his mother was speaking with her friend on the phone, Greg did all three.

Greg was different from Beverly's other children. They were blond; he was dark. They were all cartoon fans; Greg preferred the quietness of his bedroom, sometimes creating cartoons of his own. According to his second-grade teacher, Greg "marched to a different drummer." Stubbornly refusing to do homework, he finally confessed, "If the teacher doesn't know what six plus six is, I'm not going to be the one to tell her!"

Greg wasn't particularly shy; he just wouldn't talk when he had nothing to say. That alone separated him from the rest of the family. And it explained why people could never remember if he had actually been in the room. Beverly attempted to teach Greg aggression and enthusiasm for life by getting him involved in Little League. She hoped he would make some friends and come out of his shell a little during the season, but it didn't seem to be working that way. When the season finally ended, his team had finished twelfth out of twelve teams. Beverly studiously avoided the coach, embarrassed that Greg didn't care about the final score or whether they won or lost. Turning when she heard her name, she saw the coach running excitedly toward her. With her heart pounding and a consolation speech on the tip of her tongue, she waited. "Guess what, guess what, Mrs. O?" the coach sputtered. "Greg talked to me. He said, 'Bye, Coach.'" The coach turned to leave, then stopped and looked back, grinning, "Great season, wasn't it!" Tears crowded Beverly's eyes as she looked for her son. What a coach her son had—one who realized the value of an eighty-pound boy over numbers on a scoreboard!

Never forget the value of your child's natural personality. Treasure the small advances, and don't push your children to be as outgoing or driven as you. Instead, encourage them when they grow . . . in *their* time!

Perfect Parent with a **Peaceful Child**

These two share enjoyment of a quiet, low-key atmosphere and will get along well. Melancholy parents appreciate their Phlegmatic children's quiet, pleasant, agreeable traits. But they may be discouraged when this child doesn't use quiet time productively or dedicate himself to a serious project.

The Perfect parent is the most likely to motivate this relaxed child if she understands the Peaceful personality. Rather than overpowering or overwhelming the child with a strong personality, the Perfect parent is able to gently lead the child in the right direction. These parents need to be careful, though, that their standards don't exhaust the child. Remember that a Peaceful child measures all activity by how much energy it requires and is likely to quit trying if it's too much work.

Phlegmatic children need a great deal of encouragement. Melancholy parents aren't used to offering profuse praise so they must make an extra effort to take time to guide and affirm their Phlegmatic children. That's the only way they'll be motivated to reach their potential.

Your Perfect or Ours?

Peaceful children have insight like no others when it comes to the differences between themselves and their Perfect parents. Libby's two Phlegmatic little daughters are no exception. When she asks them to clean their rooms, their response has always been, "Does it have to be *your* perfect, Mom, or can it be *our* perfect?"

Libby has learned to show her girls the value of recognizing differing perspectives. Because she is willing to admit that her standard of perfection isn't necessarily *the* standard, her daughters are growing up to understand that it's okay to disagree on what constitutes a "perfect" room but that they have to agree on which standard to use in a given situation.

If your children grow up to understand the differences between the personalities, they'll be able to develop better people skills and realistic expectations of others.

Come Back to the Real World

Because Phlegmatic children can be so single-minded, it is often difficult to find something that really interests them. Once they find their niche and are enjoying that activity, nothing can tear them away, even to the point of neglecting other important matters. This can leave their serious-minded parents concerned.

Barb's eight-year-old son Michael spends his summer days in the fields behind their subdivision, playing with other kids at building underground forts. When she began to notice his wet pants stuffed behind drawers and under the bed, Barb worried that something was wrong with her son. Concerned that he was suffering from some kind of emotional trauma or even abuse, she planned to talk to Michael. When she finally gathered the courage to confront her son, Barb was relieved at his reply. "Well, Mom," he explained. "I'm having such a good time building the forts that, when I have to go to the bathroom, it's too far to walk and too much trouble to come home. So I try to hold it and then I can't!"

Phlegmatic kids don't drive themselves to perfection but they can get lost in distraction. Teach them ways, such as using watches or timers, to come back to the world when they are engrossed in their special activity.

Too Comfortable?

Comfort is a powerful emotional motivation for Phlegmatic children. But they can "get comfortable" wherever they end up, much to the dismay of a Perfect parent.

Barb's son Joe loves to come home from school, drop his books on the coffee table, and head into the kitchen for a snack. After bringing his chips and soda to the coffee table, Joe will plop down on the couch and turn on the TV. While he's watching TV and eating, schedule-oriented Barb invariably reminds him to do his homework.

Joe figures he's in the best possible position for doing just that. His homework is on the coffee table less than a foot from the sofa, so he can do homework, eat, and watch TV all from the comfort of the couch. Of course, he doesn't actually do this. After about an hour Barb will notice that Joe has taken off his shoes and socks, which are now on the couch, and has retrieved his hand-held video game and a pillow from his room. No matter where Joe is in the house, he creates his own little comfort zone, which seems like a huge mess to his mother. Almost every day she used to remind him, "The living room is not your bedroom!"

To keep from going crazy, Melancholy Barb has learned to let Joe settle in to relax for a while each day. But after a half-hour Joe knows it's time to get up, put all his food and trash away, and finish his homework. They have both compromised, and Joe is happy he doesn't have to hear "the living room is not your bedroom" every day!

It's a Phlegmatic strength to be able to make any place a little "home away from home." But don't allow your children to avoid the responsibility of cleaning up their own mess.

Peaceful Parent with a **Peaceful Child**

Phlegmatic parent and child agree that life is "no big deal." They enjoy a relaxed, easygoing relationship because they both determine not to "sweat the small stuff." At times, though, they may fall into a rut of noncommunication. If you don't put energy into this relationship, it will be nonexistent.

The Peaceful child is the easiest to raise, especially for the parent who doesn't like to expend a lot of energy keeping up with a busy child. My son-in-law Randy was so adaptable when he was a child that he would sit quietly and read wherever his parents took him. He'd sleep anywhere and eat any time.

This relaxed attitude pleases a relaxed parent, but Peaceful parents shouldn't be relaxed about all areas of life. They must also develop self-discipline and model it to their children. Motivate your children and help them set goals and develop steps to meet them.

Too Much Work

Problems arise with motivation for the Peaceful parent-child pair. Both may remain unmotivated and unmoving. Or if a child takes interest in an activity, the parent may not be supportive because it's just too much like work. Some parents are even willing to go so far as to twist the truth if it will save some effort on their part.

Ray wanted to be in Little League and dragged his father to the tryouts. A few days later his father informed him that the coach had called to say he hadn't qualified for the team. Ray was disappointed but he peacefully accepted the fact that he wasn't good enough to play. Some time later the coach told Ray, "It's a shame your father couldn't help us out so you could play." Ray listened in dismay while the coach explained that it wasn't Ray's lack of talent but his father's unwillingness to help coach or transport him to and from the games that prevented his being accepted on the team.

Ray was so depressed over this revelation that he never tried out for sports again. A typical Peaceful, Ray never discussed his hurt with his father. In fact, his father still isn't aware that Ray knows the truth. *He* certainly never brought up the subject!

Deception and unwillingness to bring up unpleasant topics strangle relationships between Peacefuls. They'll do anything to avoid confrontation, which leaves them living a life without meaningful communication.

Fun Isn't What You *Do*

Phlegmatic parents and children relax with each other and remove the pressures that others are putting on them. They can kick back in their lounge chairs or spend the afternoon fishing without concern for time or telephone.

Twelve-year-old Joe spends weekends with his divorced dad, Mike. Joe loves to tell "Phlego" stories about time with his dad.

They usually go out to dinner on Friday night at a fast-food place, because it's much easier and they never have to do any dishes. On Saturdays they get up early to go fishing, stopping by the doughnut shop for breakfast on the way. Sometimes they go shopping, but only to go in, get what they need, and go home. By the afternoon they're both tired so they come home, turn on the TV, watch a game, and take a nap. At night they'll rent a video. After church on Sunday morning Joe's dad takes him home. Though their weekends aren't exciting by many people's standards, Joe reports, "I have so much fun with my dad."

Peaceful children and parents should enjoy these relaxed times together but they must take care to not completely tune out the rest of the world. If they do, they'll never get on with life, because neither one motivates the other.

Talk to Me!

If Phlegmatic parents don't force themselves to be more responsive to the world around them, their children will learn not to go to them for action or answers. Bob remained distant from his kids during their childhood. He offered them few suggestions and functioned as if they were on remote control.

Bob's daughter grew up figuring, "If I ask Dad a question about something, I'll just have to wait about three days before I get an answer." She didn't see her dad as someone who would respond or even care. After she graduated from high school, Kara moved out of the house and went to live with her two cousins in Southern California. Bob was concerned, but not enough to say a whole lot to her.

During the next three years, Bob learned about the personalities for the first time and finally began to live in his strengths. When his daughter called to ask if she could move back home, he happily agreed. The dad she found when she arrived was very different from the one she'd left behind three years earlier.

One day she approached Bob. "Dad, you have changed so much," she commented. "You're not the same man I grew up with. I can talk with you now." Understanding his weakness at communication and his daughter's need to be understood and loved has helped Bob build a new relationship with his daughter. If you're a Peaceful parent, be sure you make the effort to build meaningful communication with your children.

Phlegmatic children can bring peace and relaxation to any home. Be grateful for their pleasant and relaxed manner but don't let them become lazy and drift through life. Teach them to take responsibility for their lives and to pursue worthwhile goals. With loving motivation and encouragement, these pleasant people will rise to the top of their game.

Presidents Eisenhower, Ford, and Bush were all Phlegmatics who set goals as children and with single-minded interest pursued the highest position in our country. They won not because they had brilliant ideas but because they were pleasant, personable, and peaceful individuals who could be trusted. Give your Phlegmatics high motivation, help them set specific goals that suit their personality and talents, and let them know that they too can become great leaders!

eleven

ENJOYING YOUR FAMILY'S PERSONALITY PORTRAIT

Understanding is a fountain of life to those who have it.

Proverbs 16:22

Once we understand all the variables that affect all parent-child relationships we can start to appreciate the unique strengths and weaknesses of the members of our own family. It's easy to think that your experiences are hopelessly beyond the norm, but remember that there are sixteen possible parent-child combinations and no two will function identically. And if you have four children, you may have four different combinations! What you learned by trial and error with the first one may not work with the others. So it's important to identify and work within the personalities of each relationship. Once you understand each family member's personality, you'll be able to look at each one separately, appreciate both their strengths and weaknesses and your own, and begin to enjoy the overall portrait.

No Two Alike

Diane's four sons are close together in age, but far apart in personality characteristics. David, her firstborn, came into the world as a cheerful, peaceful baby who enjoyed life, was agreeable in every way, and hardly ever cried. This happy-go-lucky Sanguine charms everyone he meets. Even if he never achieves fame and fortune, he will always have fun and lots of friends.

Diane's second son, Rick, was as different from David as a bullfrog from a butterfly. Rick was bombastic, noisy, and strong-willed (in fact, you might even call him iron-willed). Rick has a kind and gentle heart beneath his rough and tough exterior, but it's hard to reach his gentle side. And most of the time when he was little, it often seemed too much of a struggle for Diane to try.

Number three son, Robbie, is Diane's Melancholy. He was born when Rick was exactly two and David was almost four. Robbie peered out between the bars of the crib and seemed to be pondering and analyzing all the other members of the family. He lined his matchbox cars up in neat rows instead of leaving them helter-skelter like David or throwing them in anger as Rick often did. Early in life, Robbie decided he would one day be an entrepreneur and began to make plans accordingly. He is now the owner of a restaurant, which he runs with meticulous precision.

Diane's youngest son, Glen, was a surprise package. Born just seventeen months after Robbie, Glen was late and arrived somewhat reluctantly. He was the only baby for which Diane went to the hospital twice with false labor—which set the tone for his lifestyle. Phlegmatic Glen has been a procrastinator his whole life. He's completely likeable, even lovable, but as Diane says, "He can drive you nuts while you wait for him to arrive, take action, or complete a project."

If Diane didn't understand the differences in the personalities, she'd look back on her years of raising these diverse children as a complete failure. Instead, she can laugh with her children at situations that baffled her at the time but that she now knows were perfect demonstrations of each son's personality.

Understanding the Past

When we examine past events through the looking glass of the basic personalities, we often begin to understand things that baffled us at the time. My Aunt Sadie was a Choleric/Melancholy spinster who lived with my Phlegmatic grandmother. On Christmas Day our family would join in a big celebration with all the extended family members. Everyone brought a small contribution for the meal, but the bulk of the work was left to Aunt Sadie. She slaved in the kitchen while the rest of us thought that by peeling a few potatoes or chopping an onion, we'd done our share.

Once dinner was perfectly arranged on the table, we gathered for a feast accentuated by fun and laughter. When we finished, we took our dishes to the kitchen and left to go socialize some more. None of us even thought to thank Aunt Sadie for her work or to offer to help her with the cleanup afterward. Faced with a mountain of dishes and leftovers, Aunt Sadie would burst into tears and sob, "Nobody appreciates all I do." There would be a heavy silence as Aunt Sadie would run off to her room, then we would all pitch in to clean up the kitchen. After about an hour, my grandma would pull me aside and say, "It's time for you to go upstairs and cheer up your aunt. Tell her the dishes are done and we want her to come down." I wondered at the time why I was always chosen, but I obliged, and Aunt Sadie would come down.

As a child I didn't understand what was happening, but now I see why this scenario repeated itself year after year. Aunt Sadie's Melancholy nature wanted Christmas to be perfect, and her Choleric nature worked her fingers to the bone to make it that way. Yet she received no appreciation for all she'd done. When she ran off, I was appointed (as the oldest Sanguine) to cheer her up. And it always worked. She couldn't resist my Sanguine charm and, after she had received a little love and appreciation from the rest of the family, enjoyed socializing with everyone else. The same thing happened every year because all of us continued to act precisely as our personalities were inclined.

It's enlightening for us adults to think back on some of the family scenes that we didn't understand as children. After we've grasped the concept of the personalities, we finally understand what made everyone act as they did. And our bewilderment is often replaced with amusement!

Celebrating the Present

Although hindsight is often the best sight, you don't have to wait until your children are grown to learn to appreciate the differences within your family. Now that you understand the four personalities, explain them to your children. Take time to talk with them as you begin to celebrate the combination of personalities in your family:

- Ask each child what he or she likes and doesn't like about your family. Listen attentively and let each child know you care.
- Have fun discussing each family member's personality.
- Emphasize the positives in each personality—pointing out that one is not better than another. We all have strengths and weaknesses and we don't try to swap and become someone else.
- Compliment your children on their strengths.
- Let your children see how much better their peers would like them and their family would appreciate them if they functioned in their strengths.
- Show your children that their personality weaknesses are natural traits that need to be overcome.

- Be willing to share your own personality, pluses and minuses, and tell your children what you're working on improving. Check with your children occasionally to see if you are doing better in those areas.

When they begin to understand what makes others so different from them, children are much more tolerant of each other and grasp why their parents are so different. That will make your house a happier home!

CONCLUSION

"Now I Understand!"

Remember the family we met at the beginning of this book? The one with the excitable child, flustered mom, disinterested dad, and bewildered grandparents? I can't help but wonder how that scene might have been different if each of them understood each other's personalities.

The child was an obvious Choleric who delighted at getting everyone else under her control and watching them squirm. She was loud and boisterous because she knew that no one would stop her. She was testing her limits and they were wide.

The mother, who had been a "good child," didn't know what to do with what appeared to be a "bad child." The father, an apparent Phlegmatic, was humiliated and tried to lose himself in the menu while the grandparents wanted to make it clear that they never would have had a child like this one (after all, they were "good parents"!).

As I walked by this disrupted family on the way to the buffet table, the child looked up and said "hi" to me. I stopped and told her how adorable she was. At that comment the mother looked up and offered, "You can have her!" My response that I'd love to have such a child rated a perplexed look from the mother but a beaming grin from her daughter. At last, the child had found someone who appreciated her!

When I explained to the bewildered mother that I have written books about childrearing, a barrage of questions began. Even the father put down his menu to listen to the conversation! I explained to the family that their child's Choleric enthusiasm for life would make her a great leader if they encouraged her strengths rather than moaning over her behavior. As I suggested ways they could set limits to prevent the child's wildness, I patted her on the head, told her she was a good girl, and let her know that I expected her to behave. And she did. When the family left, the child waved good-bye to me and the mother shot me a grateful, and hopeful, glance.

As you begin to understand yourself, your mate, and your children, you learn how to work together with wisdom and knowledge. How grateful we should all be that once we care enough to understand what makes others tick, we can get along with just about anybody!

Appendix A

AN OVERVIEW OF THE PERSONALITIES

Popular Sanguines

"Let's do it the fun way."

Desire:	have fun
Emotional needs:	attention, approval, affection, acceptance, presence of people and activity
Key strengths:	ability to talk about anything at any time at any place, bubbling personality, optimism, sense of humor, storytelling ability, enjoyment of people
Key weaknesses:	disorganized, can't remember details or names, exaggerate, not serious about anything, trust others to do the work, too gullible and naïve
Get depressed when:	life is no fun and no one seems to love them
Are afraid of:	being unpopular or bored, having to live by the clock, having to keep a record of money spent

Like people who:	listen and laugh, praise and approve
Dislike people who:	criticize, don't respond to their humor, don't think they are cute
Are valuable in work for:	colorful creativity, optimism, light touch, cheering up others, entertaining
Could improve if they:	got organized, didn't talk so much, learned to tell time
As leaders they:	excite, persuade, and inspire others; exude charm and entertain; are forgetful and poor on follow-through
Reaction to stress:	leave the scene, go shopping, find a fun group, create excuses, blame others
Recognized by their:	constant talking, loud volume, bright eyes

Powerful Cholerics

"Let's do it my way."

Desire:	have control
Emotional needs:	appreciation for all achievements, opportunity for leadership, participation in family decisions, something to control
Key strengths:	ability to take charge of anything instantly and to make quick, correct judgments
Key weaknesses:	too bossy, domineering, autocratic, insensitive, impatient, unwilling to delegate or give credit to others
Get depressed when:	life is out of control and people won't do things their way
Are afraid of:	losing control of anything
Like people who:	are supportive and submissive, see things their way, cooperate quickly, let them take credit
Dislike people who:	are lazy and not interested in working constantly, buck their authority, become independent, aren't loyal

Are valuable in work because they:	can accomplish more than anyone else in a shorter time; are usually right
Could improve if they:	allowed others to make decisions, delegated authority, became more patient, didn't expect everyone to produce as they do
As leaders they have:	a natural feel for being in charge, a quick sense of what will work, a sincere belief in their ability to achieve, a potential to overwhelm less aggressive people
Reaction to stress:	tighten control, work harder, exercise more, get rid of the offender
Recognized by their:	fast-moving approach, quick grab for control, self-confidence, restless and overpowering attitude

Perfect Melancholies

"Let's do it the right way."

Desire:	have it right
Emotional needs:	sense of stability, space, silence, sensitivity, support
Key strengths:	ability to organize and set long-range goals, have high standards and ideals, analyze deeply
Key weaknesses:	easily depressed, spend too much time on preparation, too focused on details, remember negatives, suspicious of others
Get depressed when:	life is out of order, standards aren't met, and no one seems to care
Are afraid of:	no one understanding how they really feel, making a mistake, having to compromise standards
Like people who:	are serious, intellectual, deep, and will carry on a sensible conversation

Dislike people who:	are lightweights, forgetful, late, disorganized, superficial, prevaricating, and unpredictable
Are valuable in work for:	sense of detail, love of analysis, follow-through, high standards of performance, compassion for the hurting
Could improve if they:	didn't take life quite so seriously, didn't insist others be perfectionists
As leaders they:	organize well, are sensitive to people's feelings, have deep creativity, want quality performance
Reaction to stress:	withdraw, get lost in a book, become depressed, give up, recount the problems
Recognized by their:	serious and sensitive nature, well-mannered approach, self-deprecating comments, meticulous and well-groomed looks

Peaceful Phlegmatics

"Let's do it the easy way."

Desire:	avoid conflict, keep peace
Emotional needs:	peace and relaxation, attention, praise, self-worth, loving motivation
Key strengths:	balance, even disposition, dry sense of humor, pleasing personality
Key weaknesses:	lack of decisiveness, enthusiasm, and energy; a hidden will of iron
Get depressed when:	life is full of conflict, they have to face a personal confrontation, no one wants to help, the buck stops with them
Are afraid of:	having to deal with a major personal problem, being left holding the bag, making major changes
Like people who:	will make decisions for them, will recognize their strengths, will not ignore them, will give them respect

Dislike people who:	are too pushy, too loud, and expect too much of them
Are valuable in work because they:	mediate between contentious people; objectively solve problems
Could improve if they:	set goals and became self-motivated; were willing to do more and move faster than expected; could face their own problems as well as they handle those of others
As leaders they:	keep calm, cool, and collected; don't make impulsive decisions; don't often come up with brilliant new ideas
Reaction to stress:	hide from it, watch TV, eat, tune out life
Recognized by their:	calm approach, relaxed posture (sitting or leaning when possible)

Appendix B

PERSONALITY PROFILE

On the following pages you'll find a personality profile that will help you determine your personality. In each row of four words, place an X in front of the word (or words) that most often applies to you. Continue through all forty lines. If you're not sure which word most applies to you, ask your spouse or a friend to help you. Use the word definitions following the test for the most accurate results.

Once you've completed the profile, transfer your answers to the scoring sheet. Add up your total number of responses in each column and combine your totals from the strengths and weaknesses sections. Then you'll be able to see your dominant personality type. You'll also see what combination of personalities you are. If, for example, your score is 35 in Powerful Choleric strengths and weaknesses, there's really little doubt. You're nearly all Powerful Choleric. But if your score is, for example, 16 in Powerful Choleric, 14 in Melancholy, and 5 in each of the others, you're a Powerful Choleric with a strong Perfect Melancholy.

Personality Profile

(Created by Fred Littauer)

Place an X in front of the word (or words) on each line that most often applies to you.

Strengths

1	__ Adventurous	__ Adaptable	__ Animated	__ Analytical
2	__ Persistent	__ Playful	__ Persuasive	__ Peaceful
3	__ Submissive	__ Self-sacrificing	__ Sociable	__ Strong-willed
4	__ Considerate	__ Controlled	__ Competitive	__ Convincing
5	__ Refreshing	__ Respectful	__ Reserved	__ Resourceful
6	__ Satisfied	__ Sensitive	__ Self-reliant	__ Spirited
7	__ Planner	__ Patient	__ Positive	__ Promoter
8	__ Sure	__ Spontaneous	__ Scheduled	__ Shy
9	__ Orderly	__ Obliging	__ Outspoken	__ Optimistic
10	__ Friendly	__ Faithful	__ Funny	__ Forceful
11	__ Daring	__ Delightful	__ Diplomatic	__ Detailed
12	__ Cheerful	__ Consistent	__ Cultured	__ Confident
13	__ Idealistic	__ Independent	__ Inoffensive	__ Inspiring
14	__ Demonstrative	__ Decisive	__ Dry humor	__ Deep
15	__ Mediator	__ Musical	__ Mover	__ Mixes easily
16	__ Thoughtful	__ Tenacious	__ Talker	__ Tolerant
17	__ Listener	__ Loyal	__ Leader	__ Lively
18	__ Contented	__ Chief	__ Chart maker	__ Cute
19	__ Perfectionist	__ Pleasant	__ Productive	__ Popular
20	__ Bouncy	__ Bold	__ Behaved	__ Balanced

Weaknesses

21	__ Blank	__ Bashful	__ Brassy	__ Bossy
22	__ Undisciplined	__ Unsympathetic	__ Unenthusiastic	__ Unforgiving
23	__ Reticent	__ Resentful	__ Resistant	__ Repetitious
24	__ Fussy	__ Fearful	__ Forgetful	__ Frank
25	__ Impatient	__ Insecure	__ Indecisive	__ Interrupts
26	__ Unpopular	__ Uninvolved	__ Unpredictable	__ Unaffectionate
27	__ Headstrong	__ Haphazard	__ Hard to please	__ Hesitant
28	__ Plain	__ Pessimistic	__ Proud	__ Permissive
29	__ Angered easily	__ Aimless	__ Argumentative	__ Alienated

30	__ Naïve	__ Negative attitude	__ Nervy	__ Nonchalant
31	__ Worrier	__ Withdrawn	__ Workaholic	__ Wants credit
32	__ Too sensitive	__ Tactless	__ Timid	__ Talkative
33	__ Doubtful	__ Disorganized	__ Domineering	__ Depressed
34	__ Inconsistent	__ Introvert	__ Intolerant	__ Indifferent
35	__ Messy	__ Moody	__ Mumbles	__ Manipulative
36	__ Slow	__ Stubborn	__ Show-off	__ Skeptical
37	__ Loner	__ Lord over others	__ Lazy	__ Loud
38	__ Sluggish	__ Suspicious	__ Short-tempered	__ Scatterbrained
39	__ Revengeful	__ Restless	__ Reluctant	__ Rash
40	__ Compromising	__ Critical	__ Crafty	__ Changeable

Scoring Sheet

Transfer your Xs from the previous page to the appropriate columns below.

Strengths

	Popular Sanguine	Powerful Choleric	Perfect Melancholy	Peaceful Phlegmatic
1	__ Animated	__ Adventurous	__ Analytical	__ Adaptable
2	__ Playful	__ Persuasive	__ Persistent	__ Peaceful
3	__ Sociable	__ Strong-willed	__ Self-sacrificing	__ Submissive
4	__ Convincing	__ Competitive	__ Considerate	__ Controlled
5	__ Refreshing	__ Resourceful	__ Respectful	__ Reserved
6	__ Spirited	__ Self-reliant	__ Sensitive	__ Satisfied
7	__ Positive	__ Promoter	__ Planner	__ Patient
8	__ Spontaneous	__ Sure	__ Scheduled	__ Shy
9	__ Optimistic	__ Outspoken	__ Orderly	__ Obliging
10	__ Funny	__ Forceful	__ Faithful	__ Friendly
11	__ Delightful	__ Daring	__ Detailed	__ Diplomatic
12	__ Cheerful	__ Confident	__ Cultured	__ Consistent
13	__ Inspiring	__ Independent	__ Idealistic	__ Inoffensive
14	__ Demonstrative	__ Decisive	__ Deep	__ Dry humor
15	__ Mixes easily	__ Mover	__ Musical	__ Mediator
16	__ Talker	__ Tenacious	__ Thoughtful	__ Tolerant
17	__ Lively	__ Leader	__ Loyal	__ Listener
18	__ Cute	__ Chief	__ Chart maker	__ Contented
19	__ Popular	__ Productive	__ Perfectionist	__ Pleasant
20	__ Bouncy	__ Bold	__ Behaved	__ Balanced

Total—Strengths

________	________	________	________

Weaknesses

	Popular Sanguine	Powerful Choleric	Perfect Melancholy	Peaceful Phlegmatic
21	__ Brassy	__ Bossy	__ Bashful	__ Blank
22	__ Undisciplined	__ Unsympathetic	__ Unforgiving	__ Unenthusiastic
23	__ Repetitious	__ Resistant	__ Resentful	__ Reticent
24	__ Forgetful	__ Frank	__ Fussy	__ Fearful

25	__ Interrupts	__ Impatient	__ Insecure	__ Indecisive
26	__ Unpredictable	__ Unaffectionate	__ Unpopular	__ Uninvolved
27	__ Haphazard	__ Headstrong	__ Hard to please	__ Hesitant
28	__ Permissive	__ Proud	__ Pessimistic	__ Plain
29	__ Angered easily	__ Argumentative	__ Alienated	__ Aimless
30	__ Naïve	__ Nervy	__ Negative attitude	__ Nonchalant
31	__ Wants credit	__ Workaholic	__ Withdrawn	__ Worrier
32	__ Talkative	__ Tactless	__ Too sensitive	__ Timid
33	__ Disorganized	__ Domineering	__ Depressed	__ Doubtful
34	__ Inconsistent	__ Intolerant	__ Introvert	__ Indifferent
35	__ Messy	__ Manipulative	__ Moody	__ Mumbles
36	__ Show-off	__ Stubborn	__ Skeptical	__ Slow
37	__ Loud	__ Lord over others	__ Loner	__ Lazy
38	__ Scatterbrained	__ Short-tempered	__ Suspicious	__ Sluggish
39	__ Restless	__ Rash	__ Revengeful	__ Reluctant
40	__ Changeable	__ Crafty	__ Critical	__ Compromising

Total—Weaknesses

______ ______ ______ ______

Combined Totals

______ ______ ______ ______

Personality Test Word Definitions

Strengths

1

Adventurous. Takes on new and daring enterprises with a determination to master them.

Adaptable. Easily fits and is comfortable in any situation.

Animated. Full of life; lively use of hand, arm, and facial gestures.

Analytical. Likes to examine the parts for their logical and proper relationships.

2

Persistent. Sees one project through to its completion before starting another.

Playful. Full of fun and good humor.

Persuasive. Convinces through logic and fact rather than charm or power.

Peaceful. Seems undisturbed and tranquil and retreats from any form of strife.

3

Submissive. Easily accepts any other's point of view or desire with little need to assert his own opinion.

Self-sacrificing. Willingly gives up her own personal needs for the sake of, or to meet the needs of, others.

Sociable. Sees being with others as an opportunity to be cute and entertaining rather than as a challenge or business opportunity.

Strong-willed. Determined to have his own way.

4

Considerate. Has regard for the needs and feelings of others.

Controlled. Has emotional feelings but rarely displays them.

Competitive. Turns every situation, happening, or game into a contest and always plays to win!

Convincing. Can win you over to anything through the sheer charm of her personality.

5

Refreshing. Renews and stimulates or makes others feel good.

Respectful. Treats others with deference, honor, and esteem.

Reserved. Self-restrained in expression of emotion or enthusiasm.

Resourceful. Able to act quickly and effectively in virtually all situations.

6

Satisfied. Easily accepts any circumstance or situation.

Sensitive. Intensively cares about others and about what happens.

Self-reliant. Can fully rely on his own capabilities, judgment, and resources.

Spirited. Full of life and excitement.

7

Planner. Prefers to work out a detailed arrangement beforehand for the accomplishment of a project or goal and prefers involvement with the planning stages and the finished product rather than the carrying out of the task.

Patient. Unmoved by delay; remains calm and tolerant.

Positive. Knows a situation will turn out right if she is in charge.

Promoter. Urges or compels others to go along, join, or invest through the charm of his personality.

8

Sure. Confident, rarely hesitates or wavers.

Spontaneous. Prefers all of life to be impulsive, unpremeditated activity, not restricted by plans.

Scheduled. Makes, and lives, according to a daily plan, dislikes her plan to be interrupted.

Shy. Quiet, doesn't easily initiate a conversation.

9

Orderly. Has a methodical, systematic arrangement of things.

Obliging. Accommodating, quick to do a task another's way.

Outspoken. Speaks frankly and without reserve.

Optimistic. Sunny disposition, convinces self and others that everything will turn out all right.

10

Friendly. Responds rather than initiates, seldom starts a conversation.

Faithful. Consistently reliable, steadfast, loyal, and devoted, sometimes beyond reason.

Funny. Sparkling sense of humor that can make virtually any story into a hilarious event.

Forceful. A commanding personality against whom others would hesitate to take a stand.

11

Daring. Willing to take risks, fearless, bold.

Delightful. Upbeat and fun to be with.

Diplomatic. Deals with people tactfully, sensitively, and patiently.

Detailed. Does everything in proper order with a clear memory of all the things that happen.

12

Cheerful. Consistently in good spirits and promoting happiness in others.

Consistent. Stays emotionally on an even keel, responding as one might expect.

Cultured. Interests involve both intellectual and artistic pursuits, such as theater, symphony, ballet.

Confident. Self-assured and certain of own ability and success.

13

Idealistic. Visualizes things in their perfect form and has a need to measure up to that standard.

Independent. Self-sufficient, self-supporting, self-confident, and seems to have little need of help.

Inoffensive. Never says or causes anything unpleasant or objectionable.

Inspiring. Encourages others to work, join, or be involved, and makes the whole thing fun.

14

Demonstrative. Openly expresses emotion, especially affection, and doesn't hesitate to touch others while speaking to them.

Decisive. Quick, conclusive, judgment-making ability.

Dry humor. Exhibits "dry wit," usually one-liners that can be sarcastic in nature.

Deep. Intense and often introspective with a distaste for surface conversation and pursuits.

15

Mediator. Consistently finds himself in the role of reconciling differences to avoid conflict.

Musical. Participates in or has a deep appreciation for music; is committed to music as an art form rather than for the fun of performance.

Mover. Driven by a need to be productive, is a leader whom others follow, finds it difficult to sit still.

Mixes easily. Loves a party and can't wait to meet everyone in the room, never meets a stranger.

16

Thoughtful. Considerate, remembers special occasions and is quick to make a kind gesture.

Tenacious. Holds on firmly, stubbornly, and won't let go until the goal is accomplished.

Talker. Constantly talking, generally telling funny stories and entertaining everyone around, feeling the need to fill the silence to make others comfortable.

Tolerant. Easily accepts the thoughts and ways of others without the need to disagree with or change them.

17

Listener. Always seems willing to hear what you have to say.

Loyal. Faithful to a person, ideal, or job, sometimes beyond reason.

Leader. A natural-born director who is driven to be in charge and often finds it difficult to believe that anyone else can do the job as well.

Lively. Full of life, vigorous, energetic.

18

Contented. Easily satisfied with what she has, rarely envious.

Chief. Commands leadership and expects people to follow.

Chart maker. Organizes life, tasks, and problem solving by making lists, forms, or graphs.

Cute. Precious, adorable, center of attention.

19

Perfectionist. Places high standards on self, and often on others, desiring that everything be in proper order at all times.

Pleasant. Easygoing, easy to be around, easy to talk with.

Productive. Must constantly be working or achieving, often finds it very difficult to rest.

Popular. Life of the party and therefore much desired as a party guest.

20

Bouncy. A bubbly, lively personality, full of energy.

Bold. Fearless, daring, forward, unafraid of risk.

Behaved. Consistently desires to conduct himself within the realm of what he feels is proper.

Balanced. Stable, middle-of-the-road personality, not subject to sharp highs or lows.

Weaknesses

21

Blank. Shows little facial expression or emotion.

Bashful. Shrinks from getting attention, resulting from self-consciousness.

Brassy. Showy, flashy, comes on strong, too loud.

Bossy. Commanding, domineering, sometimes overbearing in adult relationships.

22

Undisciplined. Lack of order permeates most every area of her life.

Unsympathetic. Finds it difficult to relate to the problems or hurts of others.

Unenthusiastic. Tends not to get excited, often feeling it won't work anyway.

Unforgiving. Has difficulty forgiving or forgetting a hurt or injustice done to him, apt to hold on to a grudge.

23

Reticent. Unwilling or struggles against getting involved, especially in complex situations.

Resentful. Often holds ill feelings as a result of real or imagined offenses.

Resistant. Strives, works against, or hesitates to accept any way other than her own.

Repetitious. Retells stories and incidents to entertain you without realizing he has already told the story several times before; is constantly needing something to say.

24

Fussy. Insistent over petty matters or details; calls for great attention to trivial details.

Fearful. Often experiences feelings of deep concern, apprehension, or anxiety.

Forgetful. Lack of memory, which is usually tied to a lack of discipline and not bothering to mentally record things that aren't fun.

Frank. Straightforward, outspoken, doesn't mind telling you exactly what she thinks.

25

Impatient. Finds it difficult to endure irritation or wait for others.

Insecure. Apprehensive or lacks confidence.

Indecisive. Finds it difficult to make any decision at all. (Not the personality that labors long over each decision to make the perfect one.)

Interrupts. More of a talker than a listener; starts speaking without even realizing someone else is already speaking.

26

Unpopular. Intensity and demand for perfection can push others away.

Uninvolved. Has no desire to listen or become interested in clubs, groups, activities, or other people's lives.

Unpredictable. May be ecstatic one moment and down the next; or willing to help but then disappears; or promises to come but forgets to show up.

Unaffectionate. Finds it difficult to verbally or physically demonstrate tenderness.

27

Headstrong. Insists on having his own way.

Haphazard. Has no consistent way of doing things.

Hard to please. Standards are set so high that it is difficult to ever satisfy her.

Hesitant. Slow to get moving and hard to get involved.

28

Plain. A middle-of-the-road personality without highs or lows and showing little, if any, emotion.

Pessimistic. While hoping for the best, generally sees the down side of a situation first.

Proud. Has great self-esteem and sees self as always right and the best person for the job.

Permissive. Allows others (including children) to do as they please to keep from being disliked.

29

Angered easily. Has a childlike flash-in-the-pan temper that expresses itself in tantrum style and is over and forgotten almost instantly.

Aimless. Not a goalsetter, with little desire to be one.

Argumentative. Incites arguments generally because he is right no matter what the situation may be.

Alienated. Easily feels estranged from others, often because of insecurity or fear that others don't really enjoy her company.

30

Naïve. Simple and childlike perspective, lacking sophistication or comprehension of what the deeper levels of life are really about.

Negative attitude. Attitude is seldom positive and is often able to see only the down or dark side of each situation.

Nervy. Full of confidence, fortitude, and sheer guts, often in a negative sense.

Nonchalant. Easygoing, unconcerned, indifferent.

31

Worrier. Consistently feels uncertain, troubled, or anxious.

Withdrawn. Pulls back and needs a great deal of alone or isolation time.

Workaholic. An aggressive goalsetter who must be constantly productive and feels very guilty when resting; is not driven by a need for perfection or completion but by a need for accomplishment and reward.

Wants credit. Thrives on the credit or approval of others; as an entertainer, this person feeds on the applause, laughter, and/or acceptance of an audience.

32

Too sensitive. Overly introspective and easily offended when misunderstood.

Tactless. Sometimes expresses himself in a somewhat offensive and inconsiderate way.

Timid. Shrinks from difficult situations.

Talkative. An entertaining, compulsive talker who finds it difficult to listen.

33

Doubtful. Characterized by uncertainty and lack of confidence that a problem situation will ever work out.

Disorganized. Lacks ability to get life in order.

Domineering. Compulsively takes control of situations and/or people, usually telling others what to do.

Depressed. Feels down much of the time.

34

Inconsistent. Erratic, contradictory, with actions and emotions not based on logic.

Introvert. Thoughts and interests are directed inward, lives within herself.

Intolerant. Appears unable to withstand or accept another's attitudes, point of view, or way of doing things.

Indifferent. Most things don't matter one way or the other.

35

Messy. Lives in a state of disorder, unable to find things.

Moody. Doesn't get very high emotionally, but easily slips into low lows, often when feeling unappreciated.

Mumbles. Will talk quietly under the breath when pushed, doesn't bother to speak clearly.

Manipulative. Influences or manages shrewdly or deviously for his own advantage; *will* get his way somehow.

36

Slow. Doesn't often act or think quickly, too much of a bother.

Stubborn. Determined to exert her own will, not easily persuaded, obstinate.

Show-off. Needs to be the center of attention, wants to be watched.

Skeptical. Disbelieving, questioning the motive behind the words.

37

Loner. Requires a lot of private time and tends to avoid other people.

Lord over others. Doesn't hesitate to let you know that he is right and in control.

Lazy. Evaluates work or activity in terms of how much energy it will take.

Loud. Laugh or voice can be heard above others in the room.

38

Sluggish. Slow to get started; needs push to be motivated.

Suspicious. Tends to suspect or distrust others or their ideas.

Short-tempered. Has a demanding impatience-based anger and a short fuse; anger is expressed when others are not moving fast enough or have not completed what they have been asked to do.

Scatterbrained. Lacks the power of concentration or attention, flighty.

39

Revengeful. Knowingly or otherwise holds a grudge and punishes the offender, often by subtly withholding friendship or affection.

Restless. Likes constant new activity because it isn't fun to do the same things all the time.

Reluctant. Unwilling to or struggles against getting involved.

Rash. May act hastily, without thinking things through, generally because of impatience.

40

Compromising. Will often relax her position, even when right, in order to avoid conflict.

Critical. Constantly evaluating and making judgments; frequently thinking or expressing negative reactions.

Crafty. Shrewd, can always find a way to get to the desired end.

Changeable. Has a childlike, short attention span; needs a lot of change and variety to keep from getting bored.

NOTES

Chapter 1: What Are the Personalities?

1. Cheryl Kirking tells this story in *Getting Along with Almost Anybody* by Florence and Marita Littauer (Grand Rapids: Revell, 1998), 62–63.
2. Dean Hamer and Peter Copeland, *Living with Our Genes* (New York: Doubleday, 1998).

Chapter 4: Parenting Your Sanguine Child

3. Kathy Collar Miller, *Staying Friends with Your Kids* (Wheaton: Harold Shaw, 1997).

Chapter 5: Characteristics of a Controlling Choleric

4. *USA Today* (August 26, 1997).

The popular author of numerous books, including the best-selling *Personality Plus,* **Florence Littauer** has taught leadership seminars for twenty-five years and is the president of CLASS Speakers, Inc. She and her husband, Fred, travel nationwide speaking about emotional health at seminars and retreats. Littauer lives in Cathedral City, California.